And Forgive Us Our Debts . . .

A Guide to Ending Financial Stress in Your Life—Permanently!

by

George B. Moore, CPA

Cleveland Book Publishers
6000 Lombardo Center, Suite 310
Cleveland, OH 44131-2579
1-800-860-7600

Although the author and publisher have made every effort to ensure the accuracy and completeness of information contained in this book, we assume no responsibility for errors, inaccuracies, omissions, or any inconsistency herein. Any slights of people, places, or organizations are unintentional.

ISBN 0-9632783-3-9

LCCN 92-081898

ATTENTION RECOVERY GROUPS, CORPORATIONS, COLLEGES, AND FUND-RAISING ORGANIZATIONS: Quantity discounts are available on bulk purchases of this book for educational purposes or fund raising. Special books or book excerpts can also be created to fit specific needs. For information, please contact Cleveland Book Publishers, 6000 Lombardo Center, Suite 310, Cleveland, OH 44131-2579.

"*And Forgive Us Our Debts* is the best piece of work I've seen to date in both explaining the cause of financial problems and then giving a step by step process of financial self-management. A must read for anyone seeking to manage this crucial area in their life."

Earnie Larsen
Author and Lecturer

Dedication

This book is dedicated to my mother,
Alice Whitman Moore.

Acknowledgements

I am deeply indebted to:

God, who kept all His promises

Bill W. and Doctor Bob, the founders of Alcoholics Anonymous

The 12 Steps of Alcoholics Anonymous

Kathi J., who led me to recovery

Earnie Larsen, whose tapes greatly aided in my recovery

Bill Riedler who bought the first book two years ago

Lois, Meredith and Lauren—my family, who loved me anyway

My Monday Night Mens Recovery Group, gentle men who care
enough to confront me

Jane Stewart, who believed in me and put her money where her
mouth was to make this book a reality

Jennifer Opperman of JSO Creations, whose artwork graces the
pages of my book

The Understanding Yourself and Others weekend where I
learned to feel feelings and to cry

All my recovering friends whose leads and encouragement have
helped to turn my life around and whom I admire and respect

Everyone who has ever asked "How's the book coming?"

and to

You, the reader, who bought the book and made it a success.

Table of Contents

Introduction

Would you be surprised to learn that a CPA could have serious financial problems? Yet with all my financial training, I did! It culminated in a crisis that was very frightening for me and my family. Three years after losing my home and my business to unmanageable debts, the wounds from my own "financial dysfunctionalism" are still healing. I've learned a lot from my experiences and those of hundreds of others with whom I've worked during that time. This book was written to help the millions of others in recovery, who believe they are alone in their financial misery.

Part One, Financial Dysfunctionalism: Why Adult Children Always Have Financial Troubles, explains how identifiable patterns of behavior and financial consequences exist in the life of a financially dysfunctional individual. Thus, "money problems" are not problems with money but dysfunctional or irrational behavior with money—behavior rooted in low self-esteem. What can an individual do about the problem once it's identified? Plenty!

1) *The first step is to understand that each of us is the product of our childhood home environment.* We need to understand how our attitudes and behaviors (specifically financial) were acquired in our family-of-origin experience, to know how our lives were "set up" in childhood for adult life. By understanding this

dynamic, we can begin to detach from self-blame for our financial circumstances. Blaming or shaming ourselves for our indebtedness or for our (self) deprivation is useless and illogical. We must detach ourselves from shame in order to change the irrational behavior causing financial anxieties!

2) *The second step is to understand how financial problems are related to other addictions and compulsions.* Suppose addictions and compulsions, such as alcoholism, workaholism, overeating, overexercising, etc., were not primary addictions. Suppose another fundamental addiction—*stress*—existed and these other behaviors were simply ways to feed the real addiction. That would explain nicely why we face cross-addictions or multiple addictions in recovery. Debt is always present (or is the principal focus of control) in the financially dysfunctional person. Financial stress doesn't exist without debt. Debt, then, might be viewed as another "toxic substance of choice" for self-abuse. Money issues are viewed by some as constituting a core issue for recovery.

3) *The third step is to identify the various financially stress-producing roles we have developed in order to (over)use debt.* This problem is created by setting ourselves up in some highly ritualistic ways over a long period of time. But the traditional view of money problems as being lack of control with credit cards is far too narrow a view. The roles are broadly classified into two main groups: the Income-Avoiders and Over-spenders. Various roles (such as the Entrepreneur, Missionary, Financial Infant, Financial Parent, etc.) within each group are discussed from actual case histories so that the reader can identify his own behavior and, hopefully, be encouraged to change.

Part Two, New Financial Tools: If the Only Tool You Have Is a Hammer, Every Problem Looks Like a Nail!, focuses on ways to help you overcome the financially dysfunctional behavior identified in Part One. Most books on personal financial management dwell on making and using budgets. But for those of us in recovery, budgets just won't work! And neither will any other technique that addresses the "what" of money problems without addressing the "why." If the reader's personal financial agenda calls for problems in his life (because of the behavior modeled during the developmental childhood years), then money *will* be a problem! Unless and until his perceptions about his relationship to money are changed, a budget will always fail . . . not because budgets themselves are inherently defective, but because the budget is diametrically opposed to the individual's agenda.

We must dismantle the errant perceptions, the irrational thoughts and behaviors, using simple, workable tools. In order to do this, we need to define, understand, and internalize such concepts as "financial sobriety." We need to know how to plan to get out of debt most efficiently. We need to know that every financial crisis is avoidable and, in fact, self-created. We need to know how to live within (or below) our means.

Part Three, New Spiritual Tools, addresses the final phase of recovery—attending to spiritual needs. Ultimately, all recovery is a spiritual journey, a spiritual healing. Thus the most powerful part of financial recovery deals with aspects of life-changes not necessarily linked directly to money. *Three Spiritual Tools (exercises) help the reader to develop inner strength and inner peace about material possessions, to establish new priorities in his life.* These spiritual tools have been proven to work in hundreds of cases regardless of individual beliefs, concepts or relationships with a Higher Power.

Author's note: For simplicity's sake in this text, we use the terms *he and his* to refer to both sexes. In certain sections—particularly in discussions of the development of the child—it would be excessive and cumbersome to refer to *his or her, he or she*, etc. in every sentence.

Throughout this book, the author refers to God, reflecting his personal beliefs and understanding. It is not meant to persuade the reader toward any particular spiritual belief or religion, nor is it intended to exclude any reader because of differing views. Take what you like and leave the rest.

Part One

**Financial Dysfunctionalism:
Why Adult Children Always Have
Financial Troubles**

1

I Think I Have a Problem!

Macaroni and cheese . . . again! I was both disgusted and glad at the same time: disgusted to be facing this fare again, but glad we had something to eat. We drank water because I couldn't afford milk or pop. I had quit going to my morning Bible study at a local restaurant because I didn't have money for the cup of coffee. I was embarrassed even to be eating with my family; I felt as if I were taking the food right off their plates. We ate the macaroni in silence. They were as scared as I was to think about what we'd eat tomorrow—or whether we'd eat at all!

Two years earlier we'd sold our home to pay off bills that had become unmanageable. It was just temporary, we told ourselves. Kids are so trusting. We paid off the mortgage and some other urgent bills, and moved into a dump. It was a duplex, and it was cheaper, but money still seemed to be a problem. We tried to make the best of our situation and remain hopeful, but we found ourselves creeping back into debt and resenting having to do without so many things. I was so sensitive about the condition of our home that we seldom had anyone over except our very closest friends, and then only rarely.

I got pretty good at making excuses for our change. "Taking some of the equity out of our house and putting it into the business," I said. Sounds so technical, so foresightful, so organized, I told myself. Just the kind of thing an ambitious, hard-working,

self-employed CPA/MBA would say and do. I don't think I ever
believed it—I don't think anyone else did either. I didn't know
what to think or do. Relatives had begun to send small cash gifts
and "loans," and I hurt! "Stupid pride," I thought, "You'd do the
same for them if the situation were reversed." It still hurt!

Earlier in the year our two dogs had to be put to sleep due to
old age, and I was upset greatly. That's not an excuse; it's just
another fact about 1988, the year I hit my personal bottom. I kept
thinking, "Things have to get better sometime, they just have to . . .
don't they?" That summer some good friends were going out of
town for three weeks and asked us if we'd housesit and dogsit for
them. We told the landlord we'd be moving out, put most of our
stuff in storage, and moved into their home for the better part of
a month. It was a lifesaver, because we were totally broke. We
could just buy groceries without the rent and were about $200
away from living on the street. What a great example for my kids
that would have been—sleeping in the car and using the toilet at
the park—"my dad, the CPA, the financial wizard!"

That was the part that didn't make any sense to me: how could
I have this wonderful education, all this training and experience,
and be starving? After all, I owned my own professional practice
and worked hard. But after six years I was broke and deeply in
debt. And I certainly didn't want anyone to know or even suspect
what I was going through for fear of both ridicule and loss of
business. I had to keep it a secret. So I wrestled with the dilemma
of being unable to figure it out or ask anyone for help. All I was
certain about was that it wasn't my fault!

During the spring and summer of 1988, the tension kept
increasing. People I knew commented that they thought I had lost
weight; some even wondered if I was feeling ill. I smiled and told
them I felt fine, but I thought maybe I was working too hard. For
some reason everybody (including CPAs) expect CPAs to work too
hard. It was a lie. I hadn't been able to sleep more than a few
hours at night for a long time . . . and it showed. The stress and
fatigue culminated; I slipped slowly into depression, immobilized.
Things went from bad to worse. I could go into the office, but it
was a Herculean task to return phone calls, write letters, or do
anything at all. It felt like quicksand. I was sinking deeper and

deeper, and if I struggled, I sank faster. It felt dirty and smothering, and worst of all, terminal!

Somehow, by the grace of God, the money, although tight, was always there in just the right amount, at just the right time. We were able to live indoors and eat and do the things that we really needed to do. I still don't remember all the details of that most grim period. My mind has sort of blanked out the trauma and the horror, but I think you get the picture. It was just *no* fun! I remember telling Lois, my wife, that it was imperative I get professional help with the depression and stress. I didn't know anything else to do. She agreed, and I called a psychologist.

I was quite sure I was fine, really, just unable to cope with certain disappointments—like the death of my dogs, the high staff turnover at the office, the increases in business that never materialized, the sale of our home . . . stuff like that. If only I could get someone to show me how to control my reaction to these disappointments, then I'd be okay. Maybe he'd even prescribe an anti-depressant. Yeah, then I'd be okay.

It took every ounce of concentration and energy I had to get to the psychologist's office. The first hour passed very quickly and I did all the talking. Another appointment? Well, sure, I guess so . . . we didn't really get much done today, did we? The next appointment was about the same: I did most of the talking and the hour was over. Why didn't this guy jump in here and lay a diagnosis on me? Or a prognosis? Or *something?* For crying in a bucket, this was taking a lot of time, including driving, and it looked like it was going to take a lot of money, too. I wanted to get to some results, and I wanted them right now!

Somewhere along the line, I became aware of a few things I had never seen in myself before. My psychologist recommended several books for me to read. When I ordered them, I was sent catalogs for other recovery books. As I finished one book, I began another. New worlds were opening up for me. Quickly I began to understand, to see that there were other people like me. So many, in fact, that substantial research had been done and results published. I wasn't as strange as I've always thought I was. I began to understand my awful temper. Although I already felt close to God, I became aware of a spiritual awakening taking place. Money was still minimal, but somehow there was always just enough—manna,

I thought to myself. My business was heading for a crash, but another CPA firm wanted to buy it. We struck a deal which was actually quite good for both of us, and the cash I received was just exactly the amount I needed to satisfy the creditors.

Ironically, during this period I undertook financial counseling for other people who were in crisis. I remember how useful they said I was in helping them sort out various issues. I began to see certain patterns emerge. It was as if God had given me a living textbook to study, along with the intense empathy which can only come from having had the same experience. Somehow things seemed to be moving in a certain direction, choreographed in a way that only God knew. Was I being delivered from my Egypt? I had begun to turn more and more of the process over to Him, having now almost no faith in my own abilities to manage my life.

I really enjoyed the sessions with my financially troubled clients. Although I was hurting inside, it gave me an opportunity to provide important aid and comfort to them and took the focus off my own pain for a while. I found I wasn't alone. And as I shared with them general stories of other clients' chronic financial situations, they found they weren't alone either.

I learned that inability to manage money causes shame and guilt for most people. Attacking shame became the first order of business in the counseling sessions and has remained so today. That's really what this first chapter is all about. Once I was able to admit that my own personal finances had become unmanageable, I could begin to look for, and find, solutions. I had broken through the shame and guilt to see myself as I really was, to identify myself as the chief perpetrator of financial mischief in my life.

I came to understand that God was not punishing me for some real or imagined wrong from the past, nor was He testing me the way a small boy might pull the wings from a fly. It was more like the freeway had taken a turn, but I had held the steering wheel very tightly, rigidly locked on a straight-ahead course. I was running off the smooth road onto the rough shoulder. His ways were paved and smooth, and when I strayed from them, things got bumpy. When I got far away, I could crash and burn. I had to be flexible enough to follow the road, to turn with it, trusting that it was the right road. Even with some twists and turns, it would lead me where I wanted to go.

That trusting part was easy to say, but hard to do. I wanted to become very wealthy, and since I was trained to be a CPA, naturally that meant doing lots and lots of "CPA stuff," like taxes, accounting, financial planning, etc. I thought I was being really trusting when I believed God would bring me lots of tax, accounting, and financial planning clients. I thought, "Okay, God, I've got the computer and the office, You go out and get the business . . . we'll make a great team." It didn't work. For six years it didn't work. I even borrowed money, lots of money, to prop up God's failure to generate the business I needed and wanted. It's sort of hard to trust someone who doesn't deliver after six years.

My trust issues were really put to the test when I sold my tax practice. Since the money from the sale was just sufficient to pay off my business debts, there was no profit of any sort for me or my family. But the talks dragged on and on because of my objection to the buyer's non-compete clause in the sales contract. Essentially, he wanted me to agree *not* to do any "CPA stuff" (like accounting, taxes or financial planning) within 150 miles for a period of three years. I couldn't figure out how I'd be able to earn an income without relocating my family; being a CPA was about all I knew and I didn't have the money to move.

The pressure from my creditors mounted every day. My wife pleaded with me just to sell the business and get rid of the stress. The buyer wanted to move on the deal because another tax season was approaching rapidly and much preparatory work remained to be done for the transfer of the clients to his firm. I felt as though I were being drawn and quartered. My stomach was in a knot twenty-four hours a day. I couldn't sleep. I had placed an enormous emotional investment in my business, so, for me, it had come down to selling my "child."

Financial counseling was the single exception in the non-compete agreement. I could continue to do financial counseling, period. At the time, the income from counseling was not sufficient to live on, but I did enjoy it immensely and felt it might have potential. I made a decision (or more appropriately, ran out of alternatives) and sold the business, subject to the non-compete agreement, in order to stop the pain.

In reaching my decision, I reflected that, as broke as I was, somehow there was just enough money to make it another hour, another day. I felt strongly that God was very near, wanting me to accept His plan, His will for me. I turned over the controls; obviously, *I* couldn't make this thing work!

I was so distraught the day of the contract signing, I asked my wife to drive me to the buyer's offices, fearing that in my anxious state I might get into an accident. On the trip home, I felt empty—emotionally exhausted. I didn't think it could be any worse. But while this painful chapter in my life had drawn to a close, another chapter was about to begin. I was aware I had learned a lot from the experience, and I was hoping to somehow "do better next time." I was perfectly willing to allow some healing to take place and to let God direct my life and determine my fortunes.

Later that day, I had an appointment with an organization which needed some financial direction on an interim basis. Within hours of selling my business, hitting bottom, and turning my will and my life over to the care of God, I landed a consulting engagement which lasted almost a year. The position provided me with the income I needed to substantially reduce the enormous personal debts I had accumulated in prior years. I also achieved the financial stability I needed to spend time doing financial counseling, improve my understanding of the problem, refine my skills, and promote my work among other counseling professionals. In 1989, with the combination of my consulting and counseling work, my income was higher than it had ever been before—higher, in fact, than it had been in any prior three years combined.

Maybe it was coincidental that things worked out so well for me. And maybe there really is a God who is cheering for me and wants the best for me. Coincidence is boring. I rather like the idea of someone, somewhere being on my side for a change. I like the idea that I might have a friend who knows me very, very well and still likes me a lot. I have chosen to see my financial recovery largely as a spiritual recovery. I am not advocating that people find religion in order to find financial stability, but I do believe that as our relationship with our own Higher Power grows, our other needs are met (and those needs aren't always the ones we think are most important).

In this book I'll share the things I've learned about financial recovery, from my own experiences and from those of hundreds of clients I've worked with over the past few years. I am convinced that you can benefit just from reading the book, even if you don't attempt any of the "how-to" lessons I've included. But if you'd really like to get your money's worth, if you'd really like to try to achieve serenity concerning financial issues (you can always go back to your old ways, after all), use the book as a personal financial manual. Do the exercises. I promise, you won't have to learn tax laws, or accounting jargon, or any math beyond fifth grade level. After all, none of those things helped me.

Let's walk together for a little way, shall we?

Do You Have a Problem Too?

Before trying to fix anything, the first step is making sure that what we're going to fix is actually broken. ("Who, me?") I've compiled and refined a simple self-diagnostic test from numerous interviews with clients and others concerned about their financial circumstances. This is by no means a "scientific" test, but has proven to be a good indicator for many people. It should provide you with a sense of whether or not this book is for you.

Take the Money Quiz now and keep track of the number of your "Yes" answers.

The Money Quiz

Do you? . . .

Y/N . . . feel disappointed, angry, or frustrated about your financial progress?

Y/N . . . believe that most of the people you went to school with make more money than you?

Y/N . . . try to keep your financial situation a secret from your children?

Y/N   . . . support voting-age children (not full-time students) living in your home?

Y/N   . . . come from a family where someone (including grand-parents, aunts, uncles, cousins) was an alcoholic, physically or sexually abusive, or a compulsive overeater?

Y/N   . . . have difficulty adding money to your savings?

Y/N   . . . use credit cards for most purchases?

Y/N   . . . borrow money to pay off other debts (consolidation)?

Y/N   . . . borrow money from family or friends?

Y/N   . . . get turned down for loans from banks?

Y/N   . . . usually pay only the "minimum amount due"?

Y/N   . . . frequently get "Past Due" notices or other demands for payments?

Y/N   . . . buy things for other people when it means you'll have to do without?

Y/N   . . . buy things and then not use them or keep them secret from your spouse?

Y/N   . . . usually prepare your tax returns at the last minute (or late) each year?

Y/N   . . . put off balancing your checkbook for a long time?

Y/N   . . . put off opening your mail for a long time?

Y/N   . . . go shopping to feel better or "get even" with your spouse?

Y/N   . . . make promises to yourself to change the way you handle money?

Y/N   . . . have some behavior (such as eating or drinking) that you'd like to be able to control?

Y/N   . . . think about filing for bankruptcy?

Y/N   . . . live at home even though you're over 21?

Y/N   . . . pray about your finances?

Y/N   . . . answer these questions for someone else?

If you had more than three "Yes" answers, you may be "financially dysfunctional." The more "Yes" answers, the greater the probability. If you found yourself answering this test for someone else (to see how bad his problem is), you are probably financially dysfunctional, especially if the other person is your child, your parent, your spouse or some other close relative.

My definition of financial dysfunctionalism is the creation of stress in one's life by making and using irrational decisions about money. The word "stress" could also be "excitement" or "drama," but "stress" is most applicable to the majority of cases I've seen. Note that I'm saying the problem is *not* a money problem. Rather, the problem is a personal agenda for (mis)using money to meet specific non-financial needs (in this case, a need for stress). For that reason, I believe there is no such thing as a "financial emergency," except the one(s) we create! Why we would want to create stress for ourselves, and how we use money to do it, is what this book is all about.

Yes, But . . .

. . . everybody has debts, don't they?

. . . everybody has money problems from time to time!

. . . if only I had $XXX more each payday, then it would be okay!

. . . can't I even lend money to my own kids to help them get started?

. . . can't I even borrow from my own parents?

. . . who has savings anyway?

Are these or other "Yes, but . . . " questions occurring to you? Are you finding yourself feeling very angry and wanting to put (or throw) this book down? It may indicate that you need to read further but are not ready to "swallow the pill." Rationalizing (also called "denial") helps us stay stuck in behavior that doesn't work in order to fulfill some other dysfunctional need.

The most important thing to know at this point is that changing your financial circumstances is really possible. But change takes time (you didn't get here overnight, did you?), work (just reading about it won't do), and patience (because you will make mistakes). Remember that you are learning some radically different concepts now. Because of that, financial recovery will quite often feel awkward to you. Here are some helpful hints for working this program:

1) Give yourself permission to make mistakes. Financial recovery is like learning to play a musical instrument: you will make mistakes, and you will get frustrated, but you need to "practice, practice, practice" until you get the hang of it.

2) Find a "buddy" (besides your spouse) with whom you can speak openly and honestly about your finances. Help each other over the rough spots that you will surely encounter as part of your financial recovery. Consider joining (or starting) a Debtors Anonymous group for this support.

3) Recognize there is a "financial detoxification" period that must be worked through, and it may last for months or even years. Even if you begin to do everything correctly today, the disruptive consequences of your past behavior will still present problems, which you must resolve, for some time to come.

3

What the Problem Is and What It Isn't

I remember from science class how the teacher would insist we learn (i.e., memorize) all the units of measure and their relationships. Before he would teach us anything, he would drill us on conversions from one unit of measure to another. The reason became clear when we began learning theory and later application: to solve a problem (and to pass his exams), we had to understand which facts were related to the problem and which were not.

Later, in studying for the four-day-long CPA exam, I again recognized that "setting up" the problem correctly was the key to success. Solving all the problems on the CPA exam completely, in the time allowed, is impossible. The grading is based on how well the candidate has set up the facts on his workpapers to solve the problem. The assumption being that if one's approach to the problem is properly structured, the solution will be right.

We can solve most of our problems in life by using those same methods. Maybe we don't think about how we actually solve problems, but "just sort of know" the answer, or at least whether our solution is reasonable or workable. And usually this is good enough. But if we have a "flawed formula" for problem-solving in one or more areas of our life-management skills, the result is chaos and suffering. Many of us, simply never "get" what constitutes "reasonable" or "workable."

The term "money problems" is so often used that most people actually believe the problem, and therefore the solution, is measured in "money." The result is predictable: the first thing we try is increasing income or decreasing monthly payments. Does that work? Well, what's the evidence? Since you're reading this book, perhaps we can conclude that the standard approach doesn't work very well. My belief is that this approach doesn't work at all and never will. Let's learn some new terminology so we can begin to solve the real problem.

Codependence

Codependence is "any suffering and/or dysfunction that is associated with or results from focusing on the needs and behavior of others," (from *Healing the Child Within* by Charles L. Whitfield, M.D., 1988, Health Communications, Inc.). Many excellent books have been written on codependence. It's not my intention to write another, but for the sake of the reader, who may be new to recovery and/or codependence, I think some discussion is in order.

In the early years of detoxification and recovery from alcoholism, therapists and clinicians noticed that family members of now-sober recovering alcoholics usually had great difficulty adjusting to the "new personality" in their midst. While the alcoholic was active, family members had developed adaptive behavior necessary to accommodate the drinking and all its disruptions. Now, with the recovering alcoholic in their midst, they were expected—almost overnight—to change their own behavior, to "recover" themselves. They had become "co-alcoholics."

For example, anyone who has ever attended a company picnic or company party knows how difficult it can be to break through the "shop talk" to get to "real talk." Without shop talk, the relationships, hierarchies, traditions, and even humor are no longer connected to the system (the shop). Individuals become disoriented, quiet, even edgy. Want to see it for yourself? At your next company outing, try forbidding any talk about the company, the work, the clients, and inside humor, and watch what happens.

Later, many of the adaptive personality traits of co-alcoholics were also observed in people whose households did not include alcoholics, but did include other dysfunctional individuals. The term co-alcoholics had to be changed, then, to "codependents." Their condition was "codependence."

In brief, codependents are individuals whose lives are defined (and lived) in response to the needs and behavior of other people. The codependent believes that by his actions he can control what another person does or does not do (drink, for example) or what another person does or does not feel. The codependent does not know where his life and personality end and where the other person begins (called a "lack of boundaries"). Because of the lack of boundaries, it is difficult for the codependent to see clearly which events he is and is not responsible for. Indeed, most codependents have been brought up to think that everything is their responsibility (everything that goes wrong or might go wrong, that is). The label that many recovering codependents would first apply to their behavior is probably "rescuer."

Shame

Says Whitfield in *Healing the Child Within*, shame is "the uncomfortable or painful feeling that we experience when we realize that a part of us is defective, bad, incomplete, rotten, phony, inadequate or a failure. In contrast to guilt, where we feel bad for doing something wrong, we feel shame from being something wrong or bad. Thus guilt seems to be correctable or forgivable, whereas there seems to be no way our of shame." In John Bradshaw's landmark book, *Healing the Shame that Binds You* (Health Communications, Inc., 1988), he defines internalized shame as "the essence of co-dependency." It appears to me that shame is a necessary pre-condition for codependency.

It may be intuitively obvious that a person suffering from codependence has neither a highly developed sense of self or self-worth. Said another way, logically, codependents must have low self-esteem in order to so completely submerge their selfhood into that of another. In fact, much research has born out this very observation: codependence is rooted in low self-esteem and fear of abandonment and rejection. Much of this book rests on the findings of this now-classic research.

Chaos

To speak in coldly logical accountant's terms, each purchase we make should be part of some plan, some set of priorities, roughly approximating Maslow's Hierarchy of Needs (e.g., first food, then shelter, then safety, etc.). Order is the framework which must precede and, therefore, support logic. Planning and prioritizing are most effective when they are most logical; the more logical, the more effective because logic follows order. With a plan, then, our needs (and therefore our purchases) can be anticipated and prioritized because they are logical, hierarchical.

Chaos is the antithesis of order; in chaos, all events are random. Planning is impossible within chaos, so it is difficult to know which need is "next," to know how to prioritize. No hierarchies exist. Whatever is presently in our field of vision, pressing in on us, becomes the priority. Ironically, chaos is both deduced (determined to exist) and induced (caused) when planning is absent, becoming something of a self-fulfilling prophesy.

If a person has been taught, through whatever means, that his needs will probably be ignored or otherwise not met, then it makes sense for that person to begin meeting his own needs as quickly as possible. If, as a child, a person got an unending string of broken promises from parents ("We'll go to the park tomor-row"—and never went to the park . . . or anywhere else), that child would soon learn not to rely on others to meet his needs. He learns that there is no relationship between a promise and action. Planning seems futile, events appear random, and family systems (and therefore the world) become chaotic. The child begins meeting his needs in the best way he can. Not only does he learn not to trust others, but comes to believe, as Vince Lombardi once said, "the future is now." The result is that delayed gratification is not incorporated into the personality development of this individual. He is stuck in the more infantile stage of immediate gratification of needs; his patience is limited or absent. How could it be otherwise?

Perseverance

Perseverance is the ability to sustain effort through the completion of a given task, despite obstacles, setbacks, and delays. In order to persevere, a person must be able to:

1) Believe a solution to the problem exists.

2) Believe he can form an effective solution (even if he doesn't know what the solution is).

3) Believe the reward for solving the problem is greater than the price he will have paid to get it.

Intuitively, we can see that a perception must exist of a process that leads to having our needs met, and we must be able to trust the process. But if a person's foundation for learning rests on a perception of a chaotic universe (a concept generalized from his family-of-origin experiences), then processes are not reliable for him because everything is a random event. Another phrase for "not reliable" is "not trustworthy." In a chaotic world with no reliable processes, trust is not justifiable, and patience simply means never having needs met. The lower the level of patience a person has developed, the lower will be his threshold for perseverance.

Debt

To the extent that one lacks planning, patience, and perseverance, he will move toward life choices directed at immediate self-gratification. Using something now and paying for it later while feeling secure about his future is one thing. But if he is apprehensive about future security (that is, he feels his needs may never be met), then there is no reason to plan or be patient. The rule for living then becomes "Get it while you can."

In the narrow sense, debt is money owed to another person or organization. In the broader sense, debt represents the value of goods and services purchased (consumed) that are not yet earned. Lacking current resources (money), he will borrow against the future—one in which he has little faith and few expectations—and, if he's lucky, he'll simply die before settling his account!

Thus debt is really the dollar measure of the lack of our planning, patience, and perseverance. Feel uncomfortable with that conclusion? Try this: explain in detail how any of your current debts reflect your careful planning, patience, and perseverance. Pull out your loan or credit card statements and look at them while you do this. What would your life be like right now if you had waited longer or hadn't purchased this item at all? Or hadn't borrowed this money? Although it will be developed more fully in a later chapter, be sure to include in your explanation how all the interest you have paid (and are paying) figures into your financial planning. What could you have done if you had all that interest back?

4

Where Does
It Come From?

Study after study has shown that codependence, addictions, and compulsions are grounded in low self-esteem, and fear of abandonment and rejection. But I am not aware of any clear conceptualization of how these personal wounds relate to the acting out of codependence, addictions or compulsions and how the latter are, in fact, all related to each other.

In my readings, therapy, and recovery, I have repeatedly encountered the phrase "roots of the problem" being applied to low self-esteem and fear of abandonment and rejection. If several problems have the same "roots," and if one problem (codependence) is present whenever one or more of the other problems is present, then it seems logical to me that they are somehow interrelated . . . all are part of the same "growth," as it were. An image of a plant or tree began to emerge in my mind's eye. Enter "The Shame Tree"—visual symbol of the relationship between the family-of-origin, codependence, addictions and compulsions, and financial dysfunctionalism (see illustration). The following arboreal analogy takes us from tiny seed to mighty tree.

◦ THE SHAME TREE ◦

A CONCEPTUAL MODEL FOR THE EVOLUTION OF PERSONALITY/CHARACTER DISORDERS

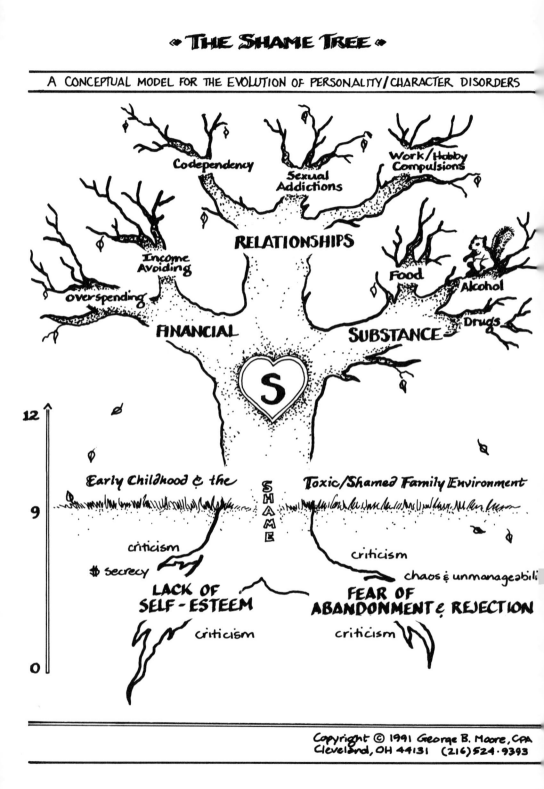

The Family of Origin—Toxicity in the "Soil"

In the beginning, as newborn babies, we were perfect little "seeds," just the way God intended us to be. Then we went home from the hospital to be "planted" in our family-of-origin (the soil in the Shame Tree diagram). Some of us were planted in very fertile, nurturing settings. And some of us were planted in hostile, poisonous environments—toxic waste disposal sites, so to speak. As we began to grow, we germinated, and our tender little roots began to absorb from our surroundings, even before we could crawl or talk. We were powerless over our environment. We just took it all in, into ourselves.

In a dysfunctional household, the family system is toxic because the individuals are toxic. The single most toxic, shaming aspect of the dysfunctional family of origin is abuse. Most people think of abuse as being physical. But I'd like to expand the concept to include verbal, physical, or sexual abuse, emotional unavailability, real or threatened abandonment, and any other (mis)treatment we received as children that made us feel somehow inferior, defective, or responsible for some problem.

In order for abuse to have a toxic effect on us, two conditions must exist:

1) Abuse must come from a power greater than ourselves (an authority figure—usually parents, but sometimes older siblings and peers).

2) Abuse must be without significant positive affirmation to offset the criticism.

Abuse Can Be Seen, Heard, and Felt

Verbal Abuse

Verbal abuse consists of criticisms, labels, curses, and opinions that painted our accomplishments, dreams and ourselves. It was as if someone had "spit in our soup," so to speak. Somehow, we just couldn't measure up, and we never would. We knew it was true because our authority figure had told us . . . and had probably told the rest of the world, too. If we tried to understand or question, we were punished. Perhaps severely. Maybe we were punished just because we were "bad." Words weren't even necessary. The message was clear. For many it was only a short half-step further from violating bodily safety, to violating privacy, to violating sexuality. And that rarely happens just once.

Emotional Unavailability

Another form of abuse is emotional unavailability, the withdrawal of the authority figure from the life of the child. The authority figure can simply withdraw into too much work, hobby, television, alcohol, reading, too many meetings, or too much of anything, just so there is no time left for family relationships. Perhaps the most illustrative example of damaging emotional unavailability was that of one of my clients. His father spoke "at most, two hundred words" to him the entire thirteen years he lived at home. In its more subtle forms, emotional unavailability is evidenced by the absence of play time between parents and children (playing ball, cards, Monopoly, or just roughhousing on the floor), the absence of any meaningful transference of skills (teaching) from parents to children, or the absence of parental interest or participation in the activities of the children (PTA, soccer, Little League, Scouts, etc.).

During the Second World War, in Great Britain, an interesting phenomenon was uncovered that serves to underscore the importance of parent-child bonding. Certain families were pulled in different directions by the war effort: the men into battle, the wives into factories and hospitals, and the infant children into day-care nurseries. In these nurseries, the children were fed and changed, but experienced few other interactions with adults. They were simply "warehoused," like so many cans of peas on a grocer's shelf. After some time, an unusually large number of these tiny infants began dying. No epidemic, no foul play . . . children simply began to die, one by one. Alarmed by the deaths, those in charge brought in more people to watch the children more closely. But the only available labor pool was older women who were unable to work in the factories. These "grandmotherly" types began doing what they knew best: they began holding, cuddling, playing, cooing, talking, rocking, and, well, *loving* the babies. The infant deaths stopped immediately. And herein lies a key point in the development of children: while they don't understand the concept of death *per se*, kids intuitively understand that parental abandonment means death, that to be abandoned means to perish somehow.

Emotional unavailability is clearly a form of abandonment of the child by the parent or authority figure. Other forms of abandonment are desertion, death, serious or prolonged illness, or divorce. The child has a natural instinct to be "connected" to his parents. They are the ones who will provide his food, shelter, clothing, safety, and nurturing. So, to be disconnected from his parents is to have these needs unmet, to perish somehow. To the child, these giants who are all-powerful, all-knowing, who can disappear and reappear at will, are the gatekeepers of life, the authority figure(s), the god(s). Bonding with them is, for the child, a matter of life and death.

Perfectionism

Still another form of abuse also presents itself frequently: perfectionism. Usually the child is brought up in a relatively well-to-do, often wealthy, family. The parents are generally competitive, achievement oriented, educated people. Alcohol may or may not be a factor in the dysfunctionalism of the family. Sometimes the parents are involved with, even heirs to, a family business enterprise or "dynasty" (not necessarily big bucks). The behavior of the parents favors the "carrot" rather than the "stick": the reward (parental love) is close, but just out of reach by the child. It goes something like this: "I see you got a 'C' on your report card. You know if you tried a little harder, you could have gotten a 'B.'" (The inference being that the parent's love and approval is conditional on, and increased by, a better grade.) The child works harder and gets the 'B.' Fully expecting praise and admiration (love) for his accomplishment, he presents his report card to his parent(s). Instead, he hears, "See what I told you? Now if you spent a little less time playing with those hooligans down the street after school, and a little more time on the books, you could bring that 'B' up to an 'A.'" Once again the child reprioritizes and applies himself. (After all, his authority figure was right about bringing the 'C' up to a 'B,' and he does feel like he must be getting closer to love with a 'B' than he was with the 'C.') Sure enough, the 'B' becomes an 'A.' Racing home with the report card, the child is still met with some emotional distance. "See? I told you that you could do it if only you would apply yourself. But look at these other grades. Why aren't they all 'A's," too? You just aren't trying hard enough!"

The child buys the idea that each successive accomplishment is bringing him closer to love and acceptance, and further from rejection and abandonment. He continues the cycle of behavior only to be met with the same response time after time. Soon he learns to play this tape for himself: "I should have had all 'A's, I should have been a starter on the team, I should have been captain, I should have been president of the student body, valedictorian, etc., etc."

Now compelled to achieve, he is able to berate himself for any imperfection, no matter how small. Anything short of perfection simply will not do. The original purpose of the behavior, to obtain love and acceptance by his authority figure (parents), has been lost in the quest for perfection for its own sake. At the same time, he has learned that relationships are not trustworthy, not attainable, not perfect. And only perfection matters. Delegated abuse!

Secrecy

Other toxic messages are imparted in the family of origin when secrecy surrounds an issue. To a child, the message that secrecy signals is "shame." Secrecy regarding money and financial matters means that money is something shameful, something we don't touch, something we avoid. In an alcoholic household (or any other significantly dysfunctional household), money is such an explosive issue that discussion about it becomes either a non-existent secret, or "World War III." The main dysfunctional behavior, such as alcoholism, almost becomes a magnifying lens focusing all the heat in another area, money. The behavior seems transparent, even harmless, in the sufficiently-delusional, sufficiently-codependent family. The "money problem" is sometimes cited as the rationale for the drinking. ("You'd drink, too, if you had my financial problems.") In addictions, behavior is always directed toward "more" (of something); the only constraint, ultimately, is that of the resources which can be converted into the "more." So sooner or later, it always comes down to money. Money (or lack thereof) is often seen as "the problem."

Financial Abuse

There's never enough money in an alcoholic (for example) household. Children's material needs are often the first to be sacrificed; a most insidious form of abuse, financial abuse, follows. In the eyes of the parent, perhaps with vision blurred by alcohol or codependency, there is nothing wrong with homemade clothes for the children, putting another coat of polish on their worn-out shoes, having hair cut at home by Mom, wearing hand-me-downs, or simply doing without.

Horror stories abound among my clients around their basic food/shelter/clothing needs as children. But the message received was always the same: "You are not worth feeding or clothing; you have no right to have these needs met because it would mean that someone better than you, more important than you, would have to do without." Some people as children, were put into a particularly cruel dilemma; the child was openly blamed as being a significant financial burden on the family because he or she needed food, clothing, toilet paper, etc. But if fruit (or anything else) spoiled, he was criticized for being wasteful for not eating it. "We all made this big sacrifice for you, getting you this fresh fruit, and you didn't even eat it, letting it go to waste." It's a no-win situation that noted author and lecturer Earnie Larsen refers to as a "Classic Double Bind." Is it so difficult to see how a child who has been imprinted (i.e., "brainwashed") with these messages around basic material needs might have difficulties making healthy choices for himself later in life?

Abuse Is the Damaging
Message about Self

In all forms of abuse, we must look at the message conveyed to the child about himself. If the message is critical of, or abusive toward, the child, then the act is toxic to the child's self-esteem. That is, the child's self-esteem is poisoned by the abuse. Prolonged and repeated exposure to this toxin has the same effect on self-esteem that a physical toxin would have on the child's body.

The Nature of Child Development—the Roots

Understanding that a child is incapable of developing a self-image independently of others is essential. Self-image, how the child perceives himself, is determined to a large extent by his self-esteem. The child does not see parental abuse and criticism as the expression of a parental problem—indeed, the authority figure is infallible—the child rationalizes the abuse as proper behavior for the parents because of the (supposed) faults or defects within himself. The more prolonged and violent the abuse, the greater the perceived self-defect(s) or unworthiness by the child. Ultimately it becomes very difficult, if not impossible, for the child to think anything good about himself, because that would be inconsistent with the behavior of the authority figure.

Sadly, it is impossible for the very young child to refute any message, good *or* bad, about himself from the parent. So, the message is completely internalized and imprinted in the earliest, most vulnerable, years. The child lacks options for leaving the situation because separation means death. In fact, when the child's self-esteem is low enough, he begins to see himself as unlovable, as rejectable. There is emotional distancing between the child and the parents that the child sees as leading toward abandonment or death.

Adaptations

The options for the rejected child center on either taking the abuse because it is "deserved," or changing himself to be someone or something lovable. (In some rare instances I have seen evidence of an older child being strong enough to reject the parental insanity and withdraw, detach, and leave the family at an early age. But I have no explanation for why this happens.) An important similarity exists among individuals, regardless of which of these options they choose. In both cases the individual is operating through an acutely diminished sense of self and self-worth. The child thinks, "The very essence of who I am means that I deserve what I get: rejection, abandonment, or any type of abuse; therefore, my only hope is to somehow become less and less, or to become someone different, or both."

The Disappearing Act

As the individual becomes "less and less" in order to hide his true self and thus avoid conflict, pain, and rejection from his parents, his personal boundaries begin to dissolve. He feels he has no rights, which his parents usually reinforce. His self-awareness begins to shut down—he is so loathsome, he avoids thinking about himself. His needs are minimized, denied—first by his parents, later by himself. A non-person needs nothing, after all. He feels nothing and becomes nothing, a "lump."

Trick or Treat

Just as one person may stop development after having become a "lump," another may take a more active role in trying to get back to the unconditional love he seeks from his parents. Instead of just shutting down all behavior he tries to adapt. As with the preceding case, his self-denial takes place first and for all the same reasons. But this person believes that there is another costume, another "mask" he can put on. This mask will not only hide his true self, but present him to his parents as someone else, someone they will finally love. And to don this mask, he simply shares someone else's identity, becoming enmeshed in the life of the other, more likable person.

Think about it: Isn't a greatly depreciated self-image, a sense of "self-nothingness," the very essence of codependency? Look again at the Shame Tree diagram. Low self-esteem, fear of rejection, and fear of abandonment are the roots of virtually every addictive and compulsive behavior. These roots are also shaped, predictably perhaps, by experiences in early childhood. This fact is important because, beyond the physiological aspects of an addiction, it offers hope that addictions and compulsions are being driven, at least in part, by something else, something treatable. But I'm getting ahead of myself.

First Comes Personality

The toxic primary relationships within the family of origin from birth through about age nine impair the personality of the child; they send messages that are damaging to his self-esteem. Based on these messages, the child alters his self-image to conform to his low level of self-esteem. If the child now perceives himself as unlovable by his authority figure, he will accept as fact that there is something defective about himself that makes him unlovable. He will begin to modify his life choices and behavior to make himself more lovable to the authority figure. Of course, it doesn't work because of the parents' own personality defects. Any rejection, in any form of emotional distancing, is greatly feared because it is the yardstick by which the child measures his progress toward love and acceptance. Now knowing that he is inherently defective somehow, he is particularly threatened by rejection because it is the precursor to abandonment (death).

As the child perceives or anticipates rejection, his frantic efforts increase to make his real self "invisible." His boundaries begin to fade, his behavior is increasingly reactive, always directed at changing the authority figure's thinking, and therefore acceptance, toward himself. No abuse is too terrible—he must deserve this! He detaches from his own undesirable self, submerging his personality into that of his authority figure and, later, into that of any other person from whom he seeks love and acceptance. He doesn't even exist anymore. He became "lost" as a person . . . missing in action somewhere in childhood.

Thus, from birth to age nine, the personality is formed. In the toxic family of origin, the personality is twisted by abuse-induced shame. Toxic shame is the sense, not of having done something wrong, but of being something wrong, of being defective. The personality that emerges has a shame core and is firmly rooted in low self-esteem and fear of rejection and abandonment.

As the Twig Is Bent, So Grows the Tree

From ages nine to twelve, behavior is shaped by the modeling acted out in the family-of-origin household. I have found a remarkable, almost direct, correlation between the financial behavior acted out by parents for their nine to twelve-year-old children and the behavior acted out later by these same children as adults. The analogy that comes to my mind is a play with "understudies" (junior actors who watch the more experienced "pros" to learn how to act their parts). The understudies are the nine to twelve-year-old children. In the dysfunctional family-of-origin household, the play is more of a psychodrama. Watching their parents interact with each other and people outside the family, the children begin to pick up behavioral cues and responses, verbal and non-verbal. Regarding financial affairs, they notice whether there is arguing, violence, secrecy, lying, cheating, or stealing going on. They learn whether money is controlled by mother or father, by the addict or the codependent. They learn who makes the money and how (i.e., honestly or dishonestly, in large amounts or small amounts, professionally or at minimum-wage, temporary and/or unskilled jobs). They learn what to say and do when someone demands repayment. They learn! And they remember.

At the first meeting I have with new clients, I ask them to describe in detail the circumstances and events leading up to their calling for an appointment. When the stories unfold, clients are at first timid and self-conscious, then more specific and full of anger. I note significant points: the couple is arguing; she controls the checkbook; he makes large, unexplained cash withdrawals; they have separate checkbooks, separate debts, separate expenses; he hoards his money and lives in a dump; he makes consistently bad investment decisions, so she retaliates by excessive shopping. They are telling me how they are acting now . . . what their script looks like.

The next step is to have each individual tell me his personal financial life history. I ask them to tell me when they recall first having money of their own, how much it was, how they came by it, where they kept it, and how they spent it. I ask that the story be told in chronological sequence, starting with the earliest period. I want to know about allowances, gifts, jobs, hobbies, junk food, comics, records . . . the whole story. I also want to know which of the recollections are real memories of actual, first-person events, and which are gap-fillers from other people's recollections and understandings. The client, in the telling of his story, becomes increasingly focused on the financial aspects of the past.

During the course of this life history, I listen for other significant events, such as the death of a close friend or relative, a family relocation, major reinforcers of low self-esteem (like always getting second-hand toys and hand-me-downs), or other mistreatment that might have had a significant impact on the self-esteem of the then-child. Patterns of abusive or threatening behavior in his childhood environment may not be perceived today by the adult as abusive or threatening because of the well-developed defense/denial system. Much pain and many feelings can be "stuffed" to justify parental mistreatment. But when talking about "money," most people are "defense-less" about their history: usually, no previous connection has been made between family of origin abuse and financial dysfunctionalism, so no rationalization, no defense or denial system, has been necessary.

Having now focused on his financial life, I ask the client to put his material life between ages nine and twelve "under the micro-scope." I want to know about the clothes he wore, his shoes, his haircut, the house he lived in, the furniture in his house, the car his parents owned, his hobbies, sports, friends, jobs, siblings, and parents. More specifically regarding parents: Who paid the bills? Who earned the money? How? Was it a lot? Did either parent drink? Did he ever hear his parents talking about money? Did he ever witness a fight between them? About money? What did they say? Who won? Did they have trouble paying their bills? Did he have to move because his parents couldn't meet their obligations or because of job changes or losses?

In the course of this discussion, it becomes clear that much of the parental behavior during the formative nine to twelve-year age period is, in fact, being acted out now by the client. As often as not, the client is stunned to hear himself telling of behavior by his parents which is almost verbatim the behavior he has been acting out himself. The point, of course, is not to build a trap or to blame the parents, but to pave the way for the direct connection between the family-of-origin messages and lessons, and the current behavior and resultant consequences.

Learning that one is not defective, that his parents were not defective, but that he is part of a multi-generational problem, creates tremendous freedom. He can now choose to stop the problem, or pass it on to his children and grandchildren. His parents gave him all they had, which was what their parents had given them, and so on. They learned their scripts well and passed on the family psychodrama to him. He learned his script and is acting it out. His children will learn, are learning or have learned, their scripts during their ages nine to twelve understudy.

It's sort of like a train on tracks, each generation being a railroad car linked to the next and following the same path as the one before it. Using this visual, you can see that he can't do anything about the car in front of him (his parents). It has already gone where it was going to go, pulled by the car in front of it. And he can't do anything about the car behind him (his children) without changing himself first because they are connected to and dependent upon him. If he wants his children to have a smoother track or go in a different direction, then he must disconnect himself from his parents and get his own car on the right "track." There are no guarantees that his children will follow his example, but if he doesn't change, it is almost certain that they won't either.

Remember the old movies where the train approaches the ravine and, just as the locomotive is upon it, someone dynamites the bridge? First the locomotive, then the coal car, then each successive car in turn plunges over the precipice into the abyss. Each car is still firmly connected to the one before it and is pulled down to destruction. If one of the cars had been on a different track, behind a different locomotive, going a different direction, it would have escaped this doom. Perhaps we can redirect your "car" to go someplace with a different outcome.

The Branches of Behavior

Return for a moment to the Shame Tree model. The branches represent various behaviors which may have been modeled for us in our ages nine to twelve era. From a dysfunctional family system, we can acquire a predisposition to any number of addictive and compulsive behaviors. In addition, we're often able to pick up, as adults, behaviors we did not see modeled in these formative years. You may have heard (or experienced) a phenomenon called "cross addictions." Cross addiction refers to the apparent development of a "new" addiction when a person successfully abstains from the "old" or primary addiction.

I can't tell you that I understand how cross addictions work, but I have a theory. In his book, *Healing the Shame that Binds You*, John Bradshaw asserts that all addictions and compulsions are substitutes for intimacy in relationships. The elegant truth of this thought can be seen readily: where is intimacy in the dysfunctional family? What happens to intimacy when an addiction is active and present? It isn't there! There is no room for intimacy when Dad (or Mom, or both) are roaring drunk, raging, abusive, or acting out in any other way. Intimacy is never shared with or modeled for the children in dysfunctional households. That's because the parents never got it. Parents can't teach what they don't know, so the children learn a life script for their psychodramas devoid of intimacy—the missing character, so to speak.

Suppose for a moment that all addictions and compulsions really were related in some fundamental way. Using the Shame Tree concept, we could imagine there was a squirrel (hence our "squirrely" behavior) living in the Tree, making his nest on one of the branches. Let's say that the squirrel lived on the branch called Alcoholism, and that we had made a conscious decision to remove Alcoholism from our lives. We would climb up the Tree, onto the branch of Alcoholism where we'd begin sawing away (representing abstinence/treatment methods, such as the 12-Steps of Alcoholics Anonymous). But the squirrel doesn't want to fall to the ground with the severed branch: he is alive and well, so he simply jumps to another branch. Perhaps it will be the Sexual Addictions branch or the Drugs branch or the Food branch, but it will be another branch, and there are many, many branches.

This word picture helps me understand the nature of cross addictions, and perhaps it will help you. I have seen it in myself. Other addicts have confirmed to me that they have experienced similar behavior after entering abstinence/treatment programs. We ultimately find ourselves attending (or needing to attend) yet another 12-Step meeting, perhaps one for every night of the week, double on weekends. Abstinence from an addiction or compulsion is absolutely necessary to recovery, but abstinence alone is not sufficient. To succeed, one must be clean and sober so his mind will work right. But if his mind is not "re-programmed" through therapy at the root level on our Shame Tree model, then nothing will change. As Earnie Larsen said so eloquently, "If nothing changes, then nothing changes!" If we want a healthier Tree, we must remove the poisons that feed the roots, not just saw away sick branches.

5

The Common Denominator

I don't know exactly how I became aware of it, but it seemed that something else was going on regarding addictions and compulsions. I couldn't explain it, but the puzzle wasn't solved in my mind. And I couldn't rest, intellectually, until I had an answer that made sense to me. The concept of all these behaviors being related made me think that they must have some common denominator. The mathematical part of my brain wanted to simplify the equation.

Perhaps Bradshaw was right, that substituting for intimacy was the denominator. But that seemed to be more of an observation about how intimacy is acted out by addicts and codependents than an explanation for the behavior itself. In any event, my belief that addictions and compulsions did have something in common was reinforced. But what?

God brought the understanding. It came from many different directions and seemed to happen all at once, but it may have happened over a six month period, I just don't know. Every week at the two ACA (Adult Children of Alcoholics) meetings I attend, the Common Characteristics of Adult Children of Alcoholics (and other dysfunctional families) is read. There are twenty-eight Characteristics in all. Characteristic #22 is that ACAs "became addicted to excitement." And I noticed that people who were coming to me for counseling were, indeed, "excited."

But stressed is a more appropriate description. By comparison, watching the Cleveland Browns play football is exciting; losing your home is stressful. Conceivably, ACAs could actually have become addicted to stress rather than excitement. I know that my financial stress took me to a psychologist. Stress. Hmm. But does that tie into other addictions or compulsions?

Drug Addicts Are Paranoid

I began to think about the drug addicts I have known, trying to see if my stress idea fit, if only subjectively. My drug-addicted friends, when not high, were as nervous as cats in a kennel. It seemed they were always worried about whether they would make the connection for a "buy," getting the money they needed to score, getting caught by the narcs, or getting ripped off by another addict. In any event, I chose to categorize them as "paranoid" (if not clinically, at least by my standards). Yes, they had stressful lives. The idea seemed to be fitting my observations.

Gambling Addicts—a Study or Two

Because gambling is clearly the addiction related directly to money, I began searching for various articles and research papers on compulsive gambling. The thing that interested me most was how little is known about gambling as an addiction and how varied the theories for treatment are. Two things became very clear to me from the information I found:

1) Compulsive gambling is *not* about winning large amounts of money because, by and large, gamblers are losers. (It really doesn't have anything to do with money.)

2) There are clear and measurable physiological changes that occur when gambling begins.

If compulsive gambling isn't being reinforced by winning money, then it must be reinforced by something else. That "something else" must be present in every case, win or lose. The physiological symptomology (what the body is doing) identified among gambling addicts includes elevated pulse, blood pressure, and respiratory rates—gambling is exciting to gambling addicts! Could the "something else" be the excitement?

Now the paranoia among my drug-addicted friends becomes understandable: suppose that all the anxiety (excitement) they had around suppliers, cops, and other addicts was the "something else" for them. Suppose that for both groups their fundamental addiction was not to gambling or drugs, but to excitement or stress.

If the primary addiction is stress, then the secondary addictions (drugs and gambling) are merely ways to get to the stress fix. This seems to make sense in light of the cross addictions we spoke about earlier: with any other illness (such as a cold, the flu, or chicken pox), when we get well, we don't expect to simply get another disease right away. If the drug, gambling, or alcohol addiction is the disease, why do we get sick again when we get well from one of them?

Bringing It Home

When I began my own financial recovery and my finances became manageable again, I noticed I was very busy working but never seemed to accomplish a lot. Other people remarked about how much coffee I drank; after hearing their comments I decided to quit drinking coffee, mostly as a health consideration. I hadn't realized I was drinking about a pot or two of coffee every day and didn't know I had a "coffee problem" until I tried to quit. Wow! Did the world go this slowly all the time? After a while, I became accustomed to moving in slow motion and the caffeine headaches went away.

I heard my wife and kids complaining about how I was always eating all the cookies and never leaving them any. I thought they must not want them because they left them around so long (sometimes for hours!). I mean cookies are for eating, right? Then I saw what I was doing: I was devouring entire bags of chocolate cookies at a single sitting. I gave them up because I didn't want to get fat (and have to spend a lot of money on new clothes). The cookies had to go.

A friend took me to task for keeping him waiting thirty minutes for a lunch date. I realized I kept a lot of people waiting—a lot of the time. I was late for appointments; I scheduled things too tightly for myself and overlapped them. Often I had to be in two places at once. I found myself repeatedly leaving the house five (or more) minutes late to meet someone. Then I'd try to make up the time by driving too fast, worrying about being stopped by the police, and making myself even later. I decided to do a better job of scheduling my time for two reasons: first, it was rude to other people, and second, it was dangerous and potentially very expensive (in fines and in repair bills if I were to be in an accident).

I noticed that the consulting work I was hired to do seemed to always be getting done at the last possible minute, on weekends, late at night, and often on the day it was due. Thank God for the computer, I thought to myself. But the projects could all have been done much sooner. Time deadlines were always very generous since I had given up my tax practice. Why was I doing things at the last minute? Why was I dragging out jobs until clients' patience was tested?

Somehow, I began to see the pattern emerge: my financial episodes were very stressful. As my finances were brought under control, I began drinking coffee because the caffeine offered the same high respiratory, pulse, blood pressure, and adrenalin levels I was able to get from financial stress. The chocolate in the cookies soon replaced coffee as the source of caffeine in my diet.

Sabotaging my time was an easy behavior for me to become anxious about: my father was a pilot in the Air Force and wanted to arrive everywhere we went fifteen minutes early. With five kids in the family, getting someplace the same day (much less fifteen minutes early) was a Herculean task. It became a drama fraught with tension, anger, raging, hitting, yelling—lots of stress-producing stuff for kids. So I simply recreated the drama for myself by poor time management. Instant stress fix!

A sub-set of time mismanagement is procrastination. Characteristic #27 of Adult Children of Alcoholics (and dysfunctional families) is "we became compulsive procrastinators." The only possible payoff from procrastination is stress!

Clearly, all this behavior was directed at creating stress in my life. I came to admit that I was addicted to stress and that, as a result, my life had become unmanageable. The center, then, of addictions and compulsions seemed to be stress itself. The addiction or compulsion both generated and medicated the stress.

Stress As an Addiction

Intimacy, the experience of being totally vulnerable, of being totally ourselves, requires that we feel safe—that we are in the presence of another person who will love and accept us unconditionally, just the way we are. That feeling of unconditional love and acceptance is one we sought from our earliest moments of life. This is the one feeling we didn't get from our parents because they didn't have it to give to us. What we sought was unconditional love and intimacy. What we got were feelings of rejection and abandonment, making us feel our lives were in peril. Desiring intimacy and safety, we got terror instead. Our parents' issues and their acting out got in the way, but we didn't understand that. As we naturally drew closer to our source of wisdom, nurturance, and sustenance, we were met with chaos and unmanageability, abuse and emotional distancing, and fear.

We wanted unconditional love and bonding with our parents; we got rejection and abandonment—a chronic dilemma. We felt deep stress from the fear and hurt over a long period. It became familiar, perhaps even "normal," for us to feel that way. Physiologically, our bodies were reacting with "fight or flight" symptomology in our times of stress. That meant we experienced elevated blood pressure and respiratory and pulse rates. As the capillaries near the skin closed down, adrenalin was secreted in huge quantities to fuel our bodies for a savage confrontation, all of which is a biological carry-over from prehistoric times. Nevertheless, it happens when we are in stressful situations.

I have another theory that stress addiction (or something like it), is developed in our early childhoods by numerous and frequent experiences with stressful situations—so numerous and frequent, in fact, that stress became the norm for us. Perhaps the addiction is to the adrenalin our bodies secreted during these stress episodes. That seems more like a question for medical practitioners. I will simply refer to this theoretical condition as a "stress addiction."

So What If Stress Is an Addiction?

Using this idea of stress addiction we can try to see how it might fit into other life patterns of behavior. Suppose we *are* stress addicts (or simply believe at a deep level that stress is a normal feeling, one with which we are very familiar and comfortable). What sorts of things might we do, as adults, to get another stress "fix"? Maybe we could find employment that is very stressful, such as a tax accountant (ahem), police narcotics officer, firefighter, paramedic, hospital emergency room surgeon or nurse, paratrooper, or something similar. By the way, how stressful is *your* job?

There are other ways of getting our stress fixes. We could procrastinate, for example, because the ultimate payoff from procrastination is *always* stress. Sure, we could even become compulsive procrastinators. We could adopt a behavior of procrastination about almost everything, from getting the report done on time to getting to work on time. We'd put off getting the car fixed, opening the mail, mowing the lawn, sending in our registration fees, exercising, spending time with the kids, filing our tax returns. Yes, we can use procrastination to get a stress fix. Actually, that's the only thing we ever get from procrastination, so it must be what we're really after. Why else would we do it?

We also can become totally immersed in controlling or changing the behavior of another individual. We can embark on a personal crusade to reform an alcoholic/addict (Dad, Mom, brother, sister, son, daughter?). "If only he would _____, then he'd be okay. Maybe if I _____, he'd have to _____." Of course it doesn't work. It never has and it never will. But the frustration and anger definitely fuel our stress addiction. The only payoff from obsessing about the behavior of another person is frustration and anger, which are stressful feelings. So if the only reward is stress, that *must* be what we're after—otherwise, why bother?

We could try dishonesty and lying. This is a great way to create stress because we don't have to wait for our "fix." With dishonesty and lying, we can immediately begin to fear getting caught. When we're ultimately caught, we can plug into more shame and guilt, which will release even more stress. Pretty nifty, huh? Two doses for the price of one. Eventually, people will figure out that we are dishonest and/or liars and begin avoiding having anything to do with us. By choosing to be untrustworthy, we will never be given responsible positions. We will begin to feel alienated and abandoned . . . feelings that remind us of the stressful rejection/ abandonment scene in childhood. We can almost see the adrenalin washing over and through us now!

Adult Children of Alcoholics (ACA), which I mentioned in Chapter Five, is another 12-Step anonymous group which branched off from Alcoholics Anonymous. ACA, addresses the problems of adult children of dysfunctional families. They have compiled a list of twenty-eight common characteristics of adult children, which I'd like to share with you here. Generally, ACA's:

1) Guess at what normal is.

2) Have difficulty following a project through from beginning to end.

3) Lie when it would be just as easy to tell the truth.

4) Judge themselves without mercy and have very low self-esteem.

5) Have difficulty having fun.

6) Take themselves very seriously.

7) Have difficulty with intimate relationships.

8) Overreact to changes over which they have no control.

9) Constantly seek approval and affirmation, often losing their identities in the process.

10) Usually feel different from other people.

11) Are super responsible or super irresponsible.

12) Are extremely loyal even in the face of evidence that the loyalty is undeserved.

13) Tend to lock themselves into a course of action without giving serious consideration to alternative behaviors or possible consequences. This impulsivity leads to confusion, self-loathing, and loss of control of their environment. As a result, more energy is spent cleaning up the mess than would have been spent had the alternatives and consequences been examined in the first place.

14) Tend to look for immediate as opposed to deferred gratification.

15) Do not appear to have any more or any fewer problems with their sexuality than the general population.

16) Become isolated and afraid of people and authority figures.

17) Are frightened by angry people and any personal criticism.

18) Either become alcoholics and/or marry them, or find another compulsive personality such as a workaholic to fulfill their sick abandonment needs.

19) Live life from the viewpoint of victims and are attracted by that weakness in their love, friendships, and career relationships.

20) Have an overdeveloped sense of responsibility to others, making it easier for them to be concerned with others rather than themselves. This trait enables them to avoid looking too closely at their faults or their responsibility to themselves.

21) Get guilt feelings when they stand up for themselves, and instead, give into others.

22) Become addicted to excitement.

23) Confuse love and pity and tend to "love" people they can "pity" and "rescue".

24) Have stuffed feelings from their traumatic childhoods and have lost the ability to feel or express their feelings, even good feelings such as joy and happiness, because it hurts so much. Being out of touch with their feelings is one of their basic denials.

25) Are dependent personalities who are terrified of abandonment and will do anything to hold onto a relationship in order not to experience painful abandonment feelings. They developed this trait as a result of living with sick people who were never there for them emotionally.

26) Become para-alcoholics, since alcoholism is a family disease, and take on the characteristics of that disease even though they don't pick up the drink. Para-alcoholics react, rather than act.

27) Are compulsive procrastinators.

28) Are afraid of success.

I felt the need to introduce some "third-party" authentication for the points I have made about irrational behavior and its relationship to the family-of-origin. Here is an organization of/for folks raised in dysfunctional families, who suffered the consequences of having been "poisoned" by that experience, and who are reprogramming themselves through the structure of the 12-Steps of AA and mutual love and support. Millions of people regularly attend ACA meetings every week. From the wealth of knowledge gained by sharing individual experiences, the common characteristics were derived. Millions of people can't be wrong, so perhaps we can learn something from their collective wisdom.

Look again at the characteristics I have listed. Can you see a pattern in them? Some of the characteristics are very child-like, aren't they? Doesn't it seem that by employing these behaviors a person could stay "stuck" in being a child/victim if he or she chose to do so? For example, Characteristic #28 is Fear of Success: "If I succeed (financially or otherwise), then I will be an adult, because adults do things right and kids screw things up; I am not an adult (and don't want to be), so my (infantile) behavior is appropriate." Similarly, problems with task completion, immediate gratification, fear of authority figures, and over-involvement in the affairs of others are easily recognizable for their childlike qualities. Does it also appear to you that the payoff in each behavior ultimately will be increased stress as adults try to cope with life using a child's skills?

So, here are millions of people who have experienced such stress as to label their lives "unmanageable." These millions have come to understand the effects in adulthood of being raised in a dysfunctional family. By identifying common behavior patterns, we can begin to identify behavior that doesn't "work." And that, in itself, is the first step.

6

Cataloging the Behavior

In dysfunctional households, family members have been found to adopt certain classic coping roles around the behavior of the centrally dysfunctional individual. For example, the Hero tries to bring honor and glory to his dysfunctional family. He becomes the all-American boy—marvelous grades, charismatic personality, athletic prowess, super responsibility, great dancer—you get the idea: "The better I look, the better we look." The Mascot is the funny "sidekick" whose role is to provide comic relief from the ever-present tension in the family. The Scapegoat is the "trouble maker," whose role is to take the family's focus off the centrally dysfunctional person; no matter what the problem (even if it's just bad weather), it can somehow be attributed to the Scapegoat.

Another half-dozen, or so, roles exist representing adaptive personalities within the sub-culture of the dysfunctional family. The point is that there are roles. Sometimes family members act out more than one role (depending on the circumstances). Sometimes they swap roles with other family members. But the roles are clearly identifiable and classifiable.

Now we are back to our "psychodrama." I believe that everyone, not just those from toxic families, acts out a part in his own little psychodrama.

Importantly, these coping roles which emerge so clearly in the dysfunctional family of origin don't stop when the child leaves home. The Hero later becomes a workaholic and presents himself as one who is never wrong and is responsible for "everything." The Mascot handles stress poorly, frequently develops ulcers, is a compulsive clown, and is usually immature. The Scapegoat is a chronic troublemaker in school and at work, often having an unplanned pregnancy, frequently landing in jail or prison. The point is that the behavior developed as a coping mechanism for stress within the dysfunctional family is carried into adulthood, beyond the family, into society—with predictable results. So the psychodrama is, indeed, a life drama.

Let's Pretend . . .

Let's pretend that a person had made a conscious choice to create stress in his life by making irrational decisions about money (which is my definition of financial dysfunctionalism). There are only two things he can do with money: get it and get rid of it. Financial stress results only when he gets rid of money faster than he gets it. Many people assume that this means "overspending." But look at the condition for financial stress again. Could we also say that financial stress results only when a person gets money slower than he gets rid of it? Yes, "overspending" is one way of creating financial stress; but what about "underearning"?

Let's stay with the idea of the psychodrama a bit longer and explore a new set of roles which might be used by our imaginary financially dysfunctional hero in his life's play. We'll write a brief character sketch, remembering that the primary purpose of the role is to create financial stress by making irrational choices about money. Any resemblance between the characters depicted in our psychodrama and any person living or dead is purely coincidental.

Now suppose our hero was primarily an "under-earner," or more to the point, an "income avoider." Yes, let's be brutal about it. Let's say that our hero, in order to create financial stress for himself, actually avoids earning enough income to meet his needs. Naturally, he doesn't want to be labeled an income avoider (because that would mean that he is really responsible for the results). He'll have to be clever about how he does it, won't he?

Income Avoidance Roles

The Entrepreneur

For those having difficulty with authority figures, the lure of "being your own boss" is a powerful one. And for those who are workaholics, having their own business provides an escape unrivaled in today's corporate world: all the affirmations from friends who understand how difficult it is to launch your own firm. They understand it takes a lot of hard work and long hours. They understand money is tight. They understand when the business fails. It's fun being so miserable when so many understanding people are cheering for you. But most of all, starting their own business provides a socially-acceptable way to avoid income.

Not all entrepreneurs are income avoiders. But for someone who wants to avoid income, being an entrepreneur is a great way to get there! I know, because I've used this one myself! For over six years before I "hit bottom," I lived in a world of perpetual wait-and-see: next month (or next year) is going to be better. *If only* the new marketing plan works the way we hope it will; things are going to be more profitable *if only* the new computer system were up and running, had the latest upgrade, had better software, etc. We'll have the money we need to turn the corner *if only* we can just land this government contract. And if the money really does start to roll in, I can sabotage things by expanding the marketing program (and, therefore, the expense), or buying a bigger computer, or getting another truck, or doing whatever I need to do in order to ensure that there will not be enough money left over to pay myself.

Successful and unsuccessful entrepreneurs are hard to tell apart. Both are hard-working visionaries, often preferring to work alone rather than as part of a team. Both are not overly-concerned with outside opinion. It is not uncommon for successful entrepreneurs ultimately to be removed from the direct management of their businesses. Investors or partners want professional managers who are better able to work within the framework of a formal organization. Whether we are talking about the inventor of the "better mousetrap" or the person who simply opens up *yet another* accounting practice or *yet another* barber shop, the fact is that more than 80 percent of the businesses opening in any year will be closed five years later. Statistically, being an entrepreneur is risky and financially unrewarding—just the ticket for avoiding income—and creating stress.

The Entrepreneur

The Missionary

A Missionary is a rescuer who is not concerned with his own well-being or even his own safety. No hardship is too great, no task too menial, no hour of the day too sacred that the Missionary won't leap into the breach. In the financial sense, of course, ignoble money merely sullies noble purpose. So money is as much an insult as a reward for the Missionary.

Perhaps this is too vague. What would a Missionary do in our society? Well, a Missionary could be a nurse, a social worker, a schoolteacher, a counselor, a clergyman . . . any work where the hours are long, demanding, and tedious, the pay is low relative to the education and experience (the lower, the better for the Missionary), and the benefits are poor or non-existent. Did you notice how many Missionary jobs are stereotypically viewed as female jobs?

I'm not saying that everyone who is a nurse, social worker, schoolteacher, etc., is trying to avoid income. I am saying that if the player in our psychodrama was intentionally trying to avoid income appropriate for his educational and skill level, these professions generally present ample opportunity to fulfill the primary agenda: avoid income. The societal "stroking," or enabling, is very strong too.

The Missionary

The Screw-Up

Our player might decide that another way to avoid income is to simply "screw up" on the job. Hey, everybody makes mistakes, right? Missing an important deadline, mailing the proposal to the wrong address, getting drunk and acting obnoxious at the company Christmas party, and coming to work late every day are some of the strategies the Screw-Up can use to be sure that he doesn't get too close to a pay raise, promotion, or even job security.

Another way to screw up is to simply not "fit in," to "drop out," as it were. When we hear the term "dropout," we usually think of the academic dropout. Certainly that is one way, statistically, to thwart income—dropping out of school and limiting potential income by limiting job opportunities. But there are other ways to drop out, or stop short of completion.

Some years back, John T. Malloy wrote an interesting book, *Dress for Success*, in which he described how different articles of clothing and different colors of attire impacted first impressions. Through careful research, he found that people responded more favorably to a man dressed in a dark blue suit with a white shirt and maroon tie than they did to another dressed in a brown suit with a pastel shirt and a bow tie, for example. Certain articles of clothing were so "deadly" in the formation of first impressions (such as the dreaded green polyester leisure suit) that Malloy instructed his readers to destroy them in lieu of giving such items to a charitable cause. Giving a green polyester leisure suit to a poor person, opined Malloy, was not a nice thing to do.

Malloy's excellent book tells very clearly that our clothing always sends a message to people (right or wrong), and the choice of the message we send is made by our choices in attire. The operative word here is "choice." If we choose to wear clothing that communicates a message to others of "untrustworthy," "different," or "stuck in his teen years," isn't that another way of "dropping out," of showing incompleteness? And if that message is going out to current or prospective employers, supervisors or peers, what is the long-term impact on our income likely to be? Malloy tells us that people who dress within certain norms are more likely to succeed than those who don't. You decide.

The Screw-Up

Dropping out can include leaving Wall Street to become a recluse in Oregon. I happen to be an advocate of simpler living but not of poverty. Dropping out is about withdrawing from society while standing in place. It's about letting things go to pot around the house, not repairing or replacing an old junker of a car, not properly clothing the children because "money just don't mean that much to me anymore." It's about "taking this job and shoving it." It's about an inability to cope with the demands of being an adult member of society and then becoming financially passive. In the process, of course, stress is created for ourselves and our families by making and using these irrational decisions about money. Dropping out does not solve any problems—it simply creates *new* ones.

The Screw-Up may well have been the Scapegoat in the dysfunctional family of origin, but the tactics of the Screw-Up are often more passive than aggressive. Frequent job changes and long periods of unemployment are sometimes explained away by characterizing employers as nit-picky, overbearing, inflexible, etc. The Screw-Up is often very competent, intelligent, personable, and, therefore, quite adept at avoiding income.

The Artiste

There are two types of Artistes: those *with* talent, and those *without* talent. The financially dysfunctional Artiste is one who insists on pursuing his craft as a way of life despite the fact that money has been conspicuous by its absence. I'm not saying that everyone who paints, sings, plays a musical instrument, or dances should make money or quit. I happen to enjoy playing a harmonica, but I know the only way I'm likely to see money from it is if someone pays me to *stop* playing.

The Artiste with talent has difficulty selling it. If the work is a painting or a sculpture, selling the piece is likened to selling a part of his body or his child. An invisible emotional bond seems to connect the created with the creator. Or perhaps the talent is simply underpriced. I have worked with a number of artistes, notably musicians, who seemed to have quite a few engagements but couldn't make ends meet. They were feeling angry and acting very "victimized." When I suggested raising prices, I could see the

The Artiste

shock. I suggested trying a small increase, like 10 percent, at first and seeing what happened. When they were satisfied that their customers wouldn't abandon them, I suggested another 10 percent increase. Some of these clients have doubled their fees and are busier now than they've ever been. It seems that their customers perceive them to be better when they charge more. Not only that, but my clients feel much better about themselves—they never realized how "valuable" they were.

The Artiste without talent probably deserves to go hungry. Get hungry, get the message, and get a real job. Do your stuff for your own enjoyment, if you must, but please pay attention to the kind of financial response you're getting. Give yourself a deadline. Look for another way to apply your talent. Find an employment agency that can help you assess your skills, identify your strengths, and direct you toward a field in which you can succeed. And connect with a therapist who can help you resolve your sense of loss and overcome your fear of success.

Over-spending Roles

Pretend now that our hero has a good income, but would rather get rid of it faster than he gets it to create some of that yummy stress for himself. By now you are probably way ahead of me, so let's get started.

The Addict

The majority of treatment and therapy for Addicts is directed toward the physiological and the psychological aspects of the addiction. Step One in the treatment process is to stop the addictive behavior—get the body clean and sober. Step Two is to work on the thought processes that bring the addict back to the addiction, over and over again. But in every addiction, there is another consequence: financial damage. Unfortunately, it is generally viewed as just another consequence of any addiction. "Of course you're broke and you owe the mob $50,000. What did you expect from a $1,000-a-day habit?"

Of all the addictions for financially abusing oneself by getting rid of money faster than it comes in, gambling is the hands-down

The Addict

winner. If a person suffers from grandiose thinking, he may think he has knowledge no one else possesses about some future event. Perhaps he even thinks that he is telepathic or telekinetic. If so, gambling is a logical path to follow.

To illustrate, how long would you avoid gambling if you awoke one morning and realized that you really and truly could foresee future events? Suppose you could foresee all the ball scores or the next lottery number very clearly and accurately? Tempting, huh? Of course you can't predict the future, and no one else can either. But you can see that if grandiosity were a dominant personality trait and the script in the psychodrama called for creating financial stress, the gambler is the role of choice.

Most commonly we picture the gambler as some seedy little man smoking a cigar and wearing a straw hat betting at the race track or shooting dice at the crap table. But many gamblers are very successful businessmen or sports figures with very high incomes. A big income requires a voracious addiction to create financial stress. (Remember the agenda? Outgo must exceed income.)

I am not prepared to say that a person would become an addict simply to fulfill a personal need for financial stress. But I am prepared to ask the question, "Is it possible that an addiction to stress (or adrenalin) is part of the addictive process?" Could it be that the addict's thinking creates such chaos, and stress, that the medication from the addiction (alcohol, drugs, sex, etc.) is used to numb the pain, allowing the thinking to go unchanged? If so, the toxic substance of choice could both thwart and enable thinking.

The Wheeler-Dealer

The Wheeler-Dealer is a different kind of gambler. The difference is that he doesn't "bet," he "invests"—in long-shot ventures and convoluted tax dodges. The rationalization for the Wheeler-Dealer's behavior is generally along the lines of "It's a tax write-off" (i.e., government-sanctioned stupidity), "Nothing ventured, nothing gained," or other allusions to getting rich quickly. The Wheeler-Dealer and the Impression Manager (below) are the two most common over-spending psychodramas I see in my

The Wheeler-Dealer

counseling practice. Perhaps this is because I am a CPA and they somehow seek validation from me for their behavior.

In my experience, the Wheeler-Dealer usually files a rather complex income tax return. Frequently he files the return on an extension (i.e., with IRS permission to file after April 15) or simply files it late. He almost always has plenty of unsolicited opinions about taxation, the IRS, government spending, and on and on. An obsession about reducing or eliminating his income tax is part of the behavior that leads, ultimately, to his financial stress.

Let me explain this last statement because, even if you aren't a Wheeler-Dealer yourself, you may be married to one, or making some of the same mistakes about tax deductions. Many people think there is something "magical" about a tax deduction—that somehow, if you have enough tax deductions, you will become wealthy. That is absolutely, positively *wrong*! Here's why: If you spend $100 on some tax deductible item, you reduce your taxable income by $100; your actual income *tax* is reduced by only a fraction of that. If your tax rate is 25 percent, for example, then your taxes will be $25 lower, not $100 lower. So, when you subtract the tax savings ($25) from the amount spent ($100), the net outgo is $75. In summary, you spent $100 and "got back" $25. At the risk of stating the obvious, buying a quarter for a dollar is not a good "get rich" (quick or slow) scheme! You will never reduce your taxes by more than your deduction. Never.

The conclusion of this little side excursion is that tax laws are designed to do two things: raise revenues for the operation of the government and governmental services, and help shape behavior in accordance with public policy (e.g., cigarette taxes, "gas guzzler" automobile licensing taxes, deductions for charitable contributions, etc.). That's it! You can't deduct your way to prosperity!

Doesn't it seem strange that gamblers go to Las Vegas, a fabulously prosperous institution, to win large amounts of money without considering how many losers it took to make Las Vegas "work"? And isn't it strange how Wheeler-Dealers believe it's possible to deduct their ways to prosperity by taking on an institution (the IRS) that only collects money, and never pays out one red cent?

The Impression Manager

The Impression Manager is a master of conspicuous consumption. He can be recognized (indeed, he's hard to miss) by his "toys." The Impression Manager drips with excessive jewelry, owns the best stereo (now "entertainment center"), has not one, but two, expensive foreign cars in the driveway of his opulent home, each with "his" and "hers" car phones (unlisted numbers on the latter, of course). He jets to New York to take in dinner and a play (or to London for the big sales), buys only designer clothes, shops in the most expensive boutiques, and so on. Mind you, there is nothing wrong with any of these things. But the Impression Managers are individuals who do these things and are unable to pay their bills. These folks may be in arrears on paying their country club dues or late with the tuition for their children's private school. They may also be without the funds to pay life insurance premiums and are probably in a crisis with the IRS about back taxes they owe.

The Impression Manager is locked into a scenario wherein his self-worth is measured by his net worth. But his distorted interpretation of net worth ignores his debt and looks only to his assets, the "toys." My experience has been that Impression Managers are usually well-off financially and often live in communities of Impression Managers. Each competes ferociously with neighbors and friends to "one up" the other, feeding a sort of community insanity. And when the money begins to run out, which it always does eventually, the facade—the act—is continued to financial destruction. Often it is accompanied (and obscured) by divorce. In the meantime, the stress created is horrendous, and totally unnecessary from a rational point of view.

The Impression-Manager

The Santa Claus/The Martyr

Everybody loves Santa Claus. The compulsive gift-giver is known to give gifts that are just "too much." When you receive a gift from this Santa and say, "You shouldn't have!" you really mean it. The financial Santa remembers everybody's birthday, anniversary, graduation, and bar mitzvah . . . and he remembers it with a very nice gift. The gifts are unusually well thought out—just the right color, just the right style, just the right thing. In fact, sometimes the gifts come in both colors and both styles, indicating the Santa's obsession with pleasing.

But, alas, our Santa doesn't take very good care of himself. His income is usually adequate, not stratospheric; and it is largely consumed by the compulsive gift-giving. Most Santas I have known live in modest or even sub-standard housing, drive very old, less reliable cars, and don't dress particularly well. Sadly, they are unable to give to themselves.

Like the Santa Claus, the Martyr is a giver. The Martyr feels his job is to fulfill the needs of others and to be gracious and noble about it. The Martyr's song sounds something like this: "My wool coat has been just fine for fourteen years. I can sew the lining back in it and have it cleaned, and it will be good as new. You take the money and get something nice for yourself." Or, "I'm sure I can get another year out of my car—I'll just have it towed over to the mechanic and he can look at it. You take the money and use it for a down payment on a nice car for yourself. You really need it with your work and all."

Santa wraps his gifts in pretty paper. The Martyr wraps gifts in guilt. The Martyr gives till it hurts—everybody.

The Martyr

The Financial Infant/
Financial Parent Syndrome

Finally, a symbiotic relationship exists between individuals I refer to as Financial Infants (Income Avoiders) and Financial Parents (Over-spenders). The Infant role is assumed by someone who successfully avoids income by being a "financial baby." This posture is supported, or enabled, by another individual, the Parent.

It is important to note that we are defining a relationship which is represented by and maintained through relative financial positions or strength. These roles are sustained over long periods of time, even though the partners may change (i.e., the Infant may exchange one Parent for another from time to time). Also, the Infant and the Parent do not have to be the biological child and parent. In fact, they do not have to be related at all. Sometimes the biological parent may be the Financial Infant. Frequently in my practice with couples, the Parent is the wife and the Infant is the husband.

Interestingly, financial infantilism can be present even when the Infant has income exceeding $100,000 per year. All it takes is a relationship with a Financial Parent whose task it is to bail the Infant out of the problem again and again and again. There are many ways to be a Financial Infant. The most common way is to remain in a low-skill or entry-level job. Sometimes additional training which would lift the baby into adulthood is skillfully sabotaged with family crises, cars that don't work, and unreliable friends whose task it is to care-take. Thus, the Infant never has to assume responsibility for growing up.

Another way to be a Financial Infant is to pursue various "get-rich-quick" schemes or jobs promising astronomical incomes with "no experience necessary." To the Infant, the something-for-nothing song has great appeal. It has almost a fairy tale quality about it. For such individuals, various multi-level marketing (MLM) programs are a strong draw. Not everyone in MLM businesses is an Infant—many people work hard and do earn lots of money. Infants, however, are attracted primarily by the minimal investment of money, time and effort, and the virtual absence of accountability—when was the last time you heard of someone getting fired from an MLM business?

The MLM is a perfect arrangement for their self-perception and their agenda of avoiding income so as to be dependent on another person. If they start to succeed, they'll sabotage it. If they fail, they won't be responsible—children always blame others, don't they? And so the Infants go through all the motions—making calls, making presentations, advertising, carrying inventory—everything except making enough money to live on. That's adult stuff.

Some of the telltale signs of Financial Infants are: living at home after age 21, being partially or totally dependent on one or more persons for having their economic needs met (i.e., their incomes are just not quite enough to "make it"), or being seemingly chronic "victims of circumstances." Another sign is going into some business venture with a relative, friend or lover where they (the Parent) put up the cash and create a job for the other (the Infant). Such business ventures are often those in which one or both parties lacks any significant experience, where no legal agreements have been drawn up prior to starting, indeed where very little professional advice was sought going in.

The difficulty in treating this particular situation is dealing not so much with the financial, but breaking the deadly stranglehold the Parent has on the Infant.

Financial Parents don't see themselves as having a problem, certainly not being part of the problem. They have the money, after all, and manage it well. It's that darn Infant . . . if only he or she would act more responsibly, get a job, get a haircut, etc., etc. The Parents can't see how they are not only enabling the Infant, but forcing them to remain stuck—trapped in the relationship—by withholding love, criticizing the Infant's attempts at self-reliance, and even shoving unsolicited funds at them (thus underscoring the Parent's lack of confidence). The pressure on the Infant to maintain the relationship is often intense.

Parents often see themselves as caring, benevolent folks who simply want to help someone avoid pain. There is nothing wrong with being caring and benevolent, or with helping someone less fortunate. However, this relationship becomes pathological when a pattern of behavior—floundering Infant/rescuing Parent—emerges. Forget the excuses or the reasons; they don't matter. Look at the pattern. What is the Infant doing about changing? Not relocating,

The Financial Parent/The Financial Infant

not going back to school, not changing jobs. Or changing, growing, and growing up?

I seldom see Parents professionally. Just the Infants. The burden, sense of failure and inadequacy eventually becomes too much. The good news is that once the Infant sees the big picture, the necessary steps toward change can begin. Learning to establish clear personal boundaries, avoid toxic relationships and pursue only healthy ones, identify personal talents and the markets, get into therapy and support groups—all these things can be a beginning. The progress is often dramatic. And the process painful. But the rewards of a healthy, productive life are worth it.

7

Why Men and Women Can't Talk about Money

Money is one of the leading causes of marital breakups in the U.S. I think I've already established that money itself is not the problem, so perhaps the problem is centered more around what women and men believe about money. The difference in their beliefs about money is what comes between men and women. Because it seems to be a broadly-based problem in our society, it must be more cultural than family-of-origin in its roots.

If we believe that adult behavior became established largely as a result of the ages nine to twelve experience, we must look at the cultural experiences for boys and girls at that age to develop answers. By seeing what boys go through in common, what girls go through in common, and what the differences are, we should be able to establish patterns that "typecast" the financial roles for men and women later on. While cultural attitudes have changed greatly in our country over the last generation, many of my clients are products of the 1950s and 1960s. That is to say, their ages nine to twelve occurred during those times. As I look back, much of their enculturation formed attitudes which bring them to my office today. I wish to use broad generalities to make my point, so, for now, please set aside specific exceptions you may have. Also, I want you to focus on the experiences of children who are now recovering adults, not on what *your* children are doing *today*.

What Are Little Boys Made Of?

Think for a moment about what boys were doing when you were between the ages of nine and twelve. Boys are learning team sports, often competing in an organized forum, like Little League. The games have a beginning, an end, and a complex set of rules, the violation of which can cause a setback. The games have different positions (like second base or catcher, wide receiver or center, forward or guard, etc.) that require different skills and different procedures. As boys play different positions, they learn not only the skills for that position—they learn what it means to be part of a team. The team wins or the team loses. Everybody has a part, a specific part, in helping the team to win.

Organized sports for boys have coaches (mentors), schedules for practice, schedules for games, playoffs, uniforms, and frequently professional role models whose exploits on the playing field (and incomes) inspire boys toward excellence. Dietary and other life management disciplines may become required at some point.

Boys who can't remember who's buried in Grant's tomb engage in replays of their games in exquisite detail. Even if a boy isn't on the winning team, even if a boy isn't on any team at all, sports represent "guy stuff." Guys can feed vicariously off other guys on guy stuff. Sports become a socially acceptable alternative to more primal struggles for dominance. Skill-building, organization and direction of effort, competitiveness, accountability, mentoring, team spirit . . . bonding is taking place.

Boys are also getting to work. They are delivering newspapers, mowing lawns, shoveling snowy sidewalks, and raking leaves for money (never at home, of course). Hard physical work. Adults admire ("stroke") hard-working boys. A connection is made between how hard and how long a boy works and how much money he makes. As a boy masters a particular task, he is given one with a little more responsibility. More responsibility leads to more money. More money means a boy can get more of the things he wants (baseball cards, a better glove, better cleats or sneakers, a better bike, a stereo and, later, better dates with girls). He is able to make himself happy with the stuff he gets. Getting more of the things he wants means more autonomy, more, well, *power*. Hmm. Work equals money equals more toys equals happiness equals power. Work equals happiness. Money equals power.

Just as with sports, even if a boy doesn't have a job himself, earning money by working hard represents guy stuff. And guys can feed vicariously off other guys on guy stuff. Work becomes another socially acceptable alternative to struggles for dominance.

Guys learn that over some period of time they will acquire increasing skills and therefore increasing responsibility and therefore increasing amounts of money. After-school and summer jobs are progressively more interesting, challenging, and financially rewarding. Work appears to follow a stairstep pattern upward, much as do sports. Build skills and succeed, step by step. Money comes in ever-increasing amounts.

What Are Little Girls Made Of?

Girls ages nine to twelve undergo completely different enculturation about working, networking, and money. In general, girls this age have few, if any, team sports. Anyway, girls are taught to let the boys win. Athletic ability, like intellectual ability, is seen as unfeminine (mostly by other girls). Competition among girls is directed toward appearances and being popular. Popularity is important for girls because it is a basis of power. Boys may get into fights, but when the fight is over, it's over—the relationship is clear. Girls withhold relationships, so the more popular the girl, the more powerful a weapon withholding becomes. The competition is ultimately focused on attracting the most successful boy. Since girls have no basis for self-worth, being excluded from sports and intellectual pursuits, they live vicariously from the successes of the boys.

Let's talk about working. What do girls generally have as work experiences? Normally, babysitting is about all. Other skills being developed may include cooking, sewing and cleaning, but notice that these are isolated, caretaking roles on which society places little economic value. Later, when girls start to date, they have to give up babysitting because it is normally done on Friday and Saturday nights, the main date nights. Thus, a girl's economic status, her economic identity, is subordinated to her social acceptance. Her choices are to have her identity established by her acceptability to men (have a date) or have her identity established by her work (caretaking, isolated and low-paying). Does it sound like a no-win situation to you?

Let's just recap: boys are learning about working in teams, about being competitive, about working hard to make money—that money is power and money comes in increasing amounts over time. Girls are learning to compete individually with each other on the basis of things over which they have little control (looks), to draw their status from the boy(s) they attract, and to work in isolation as caretakers for crummy wages. Basically, girls are learning that sports, smarts, and money are supposed to be left to the boys.

Now let's fast-forward the tapes of Bill and Jane to their adulthood. Bill and Jane are having major fights over money and neither of them can figure out why. There are two fundamental reasons why men and women fight over money: perception and power.

Perception

Let's say that Bill and Jane have $30,000 in debt. Bill has followed the stereotypical development pattern for men, stair-stepping up each level of responsibility from boyhood with the corresponding increases in wages. As a result of Bill's beliefs that money will come in ever-increasing amounts, he has a threshold for fear of debt of, say, $50,000. That is, Bill will not be worried about his debts until they reach $50,000. From his vantage point, he doesn't see $30,000 as a problem (even if it really is).

Jane, on the other hand, does not have the stairsteps Bill had. She babysat when she was younger, but gave it up to start dating. The last "step" she completed was babysitting for $.50 per hour. That's her frame of reference, more or less, for her money perceptions. She, therefore, has a very small permission level around money, including debt. If her threshold for fear of debt is, say, $3,000, she will be freaking out about $30,000 in debt. She may be thinking that she would have to babysit China for six months to pay off the debt. She is genuinely upset!

Now Jane tries to express her views and concerns about the debt to Bill. How is Bill going to perceive Jane, based on his perception of the debt? How is Jane going to perceive Bill based on his predictable response? She'll be seen as hysterical, he'll be seen as uncaring or in denial. Who's right? It doesn't matter. The point is that no problem will be solved until it is seen as a problem. The real problem is that there is not a common language, a common perspective, a common plan.

Power

During the enculturation process in the ages nine to twelve years, boys are taught to pay an enormous price for being a man. The price is paid in feelings. In sports and in hard work, "No pain, no gain" is a recurring theme. The corollary, "Crying is for sissies" sets men up for living in pain, but never showing it, denying its existence. Never ask for help—death before surrender.

The skill-building part, because it moves men closer to money, which equals power, emphasizes competence. Never hesitate. Never show fear. So what does all this have to do with money discussions between spouses?

A woman drives down the road, runs over a nail and gets a flat tire. She'll pull over, look at the tire and say, "I have a flat tire; I need to change the tire or get help." A man drives down the road, runs over a nail, and gets a flat tire. He'll pull over, look at the tire and say, "I have a flat tire; I need to change the tire or get help." A woman takes the wrong exit from the freeway and gets lost. She'll stop at a service station and ask for directions. A man takes the wrong exit from the freeway and gets lost. He will *never* stop and ask for help. He knows *exactly* where he is! He's just taking a different route. Hours later, nearly out of gas, he may pull into a gas station (since he now has a reason) asking, nonchalantly, "How long has this place been here?" As if he knew where "this place" was.

Being lost is being incompetent, it is being weak—getting lost is something women do, therefore it is not manly. It's in the "manly manual" not to ask for help or directions, y'know. (Someone once said that Moses was lost for 40 years because he wouldn't stop and ask for directions.)

Here are Jane and Bill having money problems. Bill knows everything about money and taxes. That's because he's a man, and men are supposed to know all that stuff. Strike that—men know all that stuff. Their money problems are either being caused by external forces beyond Bill's control or it's because Jane is spending too much on make-up. It can't possibly be that Bill is lost.

Jane thinks things should be done differently, but after all, she's only a woman. She was never good at math or algebra, so how could she possibly have a credible position on money matters? Since she knows that she is genetically defective in handling money, if a problem arises, it's no problem for her to ask for help.

When the problems get bad enough and Jane has answered the last angry call from creditors or collectors, she wants to know why Bill doesn't just ask for directions. She confronts Bill with her view that there is a serious money problem. She shows him shut-off notices and repossession notices. "We have a money problem," she says.

Bill, like other men, has had money, sex, and power woven into a single strand called "masculinity" over the course of his enculturation process. He doesn't hear "money problem." He hears, "Bill, you have a masculinity problem—you are financially impotent." Rrr! This knight in shining armor drops his helmet visor, picks up his shield, draws his sword, and is ready to do battle to the death. The dragon he is prepared to slay is his wife.

Until men can unravel their misconception about money, sex and power being all one-in-the-same, meaningful discussion is almost impossible. To begin unraveling, detachment from the shame and guilt about financial problems is an essential first step. Ironically, women seem to me to have an uncanny knack for making the right financial choices. They are careful planners and, because of being excluded from the inner circles of high finance, haven't had their heads filled with the financial hogwash men carry around. As a result, women think very clearly, unfettered with complicated terminology and concepts. They are also very responsive to suggestions for change around finances and execute new plans very well.

There's only one problem for women—they don't believe they are as powerful, as competent, as perceptive as they are, so they subordinate their considerable skills to some man (husband or father or brother). Unfortunately, most men are not particularly adept at finances because they've learned what they know by talking to other men who don't know what they are talking about. But of course, they weren't lost either. (Sigh.)

Part Two

New Financial Tools: If the Only
Tool You Have is a Hammer,
Every Problem Looks Like a Nail!

What follows is a step-by-step approach to building the financial
house we have so long wanted to get in order.

8

Surveying the Property

This is about identifying those aspects of your life (including family-of-origin) that are influencing your dysfunctional financial decision-making. It is about identifying specific dysfunctional decisions, and relating your observations to the Shame Tree construct in order to have a working "overview."

To do your survey, you'll need a trustworthy friend, a tape recorder, a therapist or a journal. Or you may choose some combination of written and oral surveying. The key is that it must be complete and factual in every detail. "Factual" here means relating the facts as you perceived them and as you recall them as opposed to interpreting or qualifying them. Complete honesty is required.

The survey begins with a sequential telling of your life story in terms of money. It is *not* a resume or a job history. It is important to note your age (not the school grade level or the calendar year) when a specific event took place. For example, my life's financial story starts something like this:

When I was 6 years old, my parents decided to give me an allowance of 25 cents a week. My mother would give me a quarter on Friday evening. She got the money from my father. I put the money in an old sock on my dresser until I had saved up a little. I took the money to the corner drugstore, about two blocks away, and went directly to the

*magazine rack. There I picked out a comic book I really
wanted to buy and put it under my arm. I'd read all the
other comic books except the one under my arm, which I
then bought. I'd also stop at the soda fountain and buy
myself a milkshake or a banana split before heading home
to read my comic.*

Notice how this paragraph has factual details regarding my age,
the amount of money involved, how I got it, and what I did with
it. Not all your financial experiences will involve money you
received, however. Many will involve your parents and siblings.
Perhaps when you were, say, eight years old, you moved because
your father changed jobs, or because your parents divorced, or
because you were evicted for not paying the rent. Moving can
always be related to some economic change. A parent being laid
off, fired, dying, leaving, divorcing, getting a raise or promotion,
or changing jobs similarly leaves an economic imprint on the
children in the family. So do the births, deaths and graduations of
siblings, and relatives moving into, or out of, your home.

Although you may skip around the years when telling your
story, ultimately the incidents need to be structured in some
chronological way. Keeping the story chronological while telling
it has additional benefits in that it allows you to pull up more
detail. If you are journaling, I suggest you use a separate piece of
paper for each age (paper is cheap). This will allow you to add
additional recollections to your age-specific journal when they
occur to you. When clients are telling me their stories, I take notes
and put three years to a page. My notes are rather cryptic and
journaling will be more detailed, no doubt.

I also suggest you do all your story, whether journaling or not,
in one session. It is important to get into a "stream of conscious-
ness" mode, becoming increasingly focused, because a lot of
peripheral "stuff" often comes up while doing this exercise. I have
found that a single session just seems to work better. If you are
telling your story to a friend or to your therapist, allow yourself
about two to three hours to be complete. I know it sounds like a
long time, but you will be surprised how much you have to say.
Especially if you are honest and factual.

If someone has chosen you to be the friend or the therapist who listens to their story, your job is extremely important. First, you should take good notes because you will want to refer to them later in the analytical phase. You will not remember all the phrases the client uses, so write them down. I listen carefully for phrases about self and about money that sound like "old tapes" playing. You know, eternal truths like "our family just never has money" or "I wasn't allowed to keep the money I made."

Second, you will want to help the client stay focused, clear, and honest. If you are the client's friend, often there is a great temptation to engage in conversation or to comfort when memories are painful. Or you may attempt to analyze what is going on while the story is being told (i.e., to fix the problem right away). You will be most helpful when you are silent. The more you say, the less ownership of the history the client will have. You may even sidetrack the process with your comments. So shut up and listen.

If the client begins talking about events that are not relevant, gently guide him back to the last relevant statement or ask, "What happened next?" Men seem to be particularly adept at talking about their professions (especially medical professionals) or their military service in great detail, perhaps to avoid having to deal with painful or embarrassing accounts of financial "failure." Men also seem to want to give a job history, starting at about age sixteen, instead of a life story. What should be obvious is that men want to operate from a position of strength and competence, that men will try to control the conversation to do so, and, if necessary, lie about or omit facts that might reveal them to be weak or "failures." My guess is that a man should be listening to another man's story and gently, but firmly, confront the client on his dishonesty.

Get facts! Get salaries, get reasons for employment separation. Can the client remember wages earned? Does the client have recall of dollar amounts paid for things like the first car, the first home, etc. If not, it's okay, but isn't that interesting? For many of my clients, this is the first time they are aware of an aversion to "knowing" anything. We simply label the phenomenon as "interesting" and keep moving.

Third, if the client is married (in any sense of the word), having the spouse or "significant other" present to tell his or her story at the same time is very helpful. It helps in several ways: it allows each partner to better understand the background of the other in a way that few couples have explored in any depth. It reveals the dynamics between the two that make finances such a struggle. It lessens the tension around talking about money, and it often clarifies the truth by having another witness to the facts present. (Women seem to be particularly useful in revealing their spouse's "convenient memory.") In the process it becomes clear that the problem is not just with one person, but that it is a collaborative effort.

Also, when working with couples, I ask the woman to talk first about her history. The reason is that, in general, women seem to be more at ease talking about money, and they have more access to details and feelings than most men. By having the woman begin, a model for appropriate detail, honesty, feelings and comfort level will have been established for the man to follow. It works.

Having completed a personal financial history from the earliest recollections about money to the present day, we are now ready for the final phase. In this last step of telling your story, you will focus on the period in your life between the ages of nine and twelve (usually grades four through seven). My theory is that our ages nine to twelve experience is where we acquire our adult life skills—in much the same way that an understudy in a play learns not only the lines in the script, but the voice inflections, timing, body movements, and gestures of the actor. We watch Mom and Dad acting out their life dramas and we learn. I believe this learning is age-specific and that it is filtered through our own self-image and self-esteem, which were shaped in the first nine years of life. Having heard hundreds and hundreds of stories, I am confident of this.

Being a visual person myself, I ask my clients to pretend that they are showing a home movie about this period in their lives. It's in black and white (which is very appropriate for adult children) and the movie reel is made up of a number of smaller reels that have been spliced together in no particular order. As the movie progresses, they are asked to imagine that someone had made these movies by following them around, so that the movie documented what the clients saw and went through. They will see "projected" on the wall of my office pictures of the outside of their home, the inside of their home, their family's interactions, their car, their vacations, themselves playing in their yard, themselves in school, their parents talking (or not) or fighting about money. They can notice who paid (or didn't pay) the bills in the family, who made the money, how much money was earned, how it was earned (honestly or dishonestly, hourly or salary or commissions), how the money was spent, and how the decisions were made. This film will show how they obtained money and things, whether they had an allowance, whether it was large or small or just okay, whether they worked for money, how much control they had over the money they earned, whether they stole things from stores (just about everybody has as a child, and it still bothers us as adults), and whether they chose their purchases or whether Mom or Dad always picked things out for them. It's a very interesting home movie, unlike most I have seen.

While "watching" this home movie, I look for events and circumstances which left a message, an imprint about how to (mis)handle money. It is during this period in life that we learn our money messages and our money behavior (among other things), so it is extremely important in understanding the present. What our parents did with money, how they resolved their financial problems—or how they created their financial problems—is the leading indicator of how we will manage our financial affairs as adults. How our parents treated us financially tells us clearly how we will treat ourselves.

The matching of the ages nine to twelve experiences to the current life events of the client is one of the most amazing phenomena I have ever encountered. Clients telling me their ages nine to twelve stories have often stopped mid-sentence and burst into tears as they realize how their financial lives have exactly duplicated the lives their parents exemplified for them. If the parents fought about money, the clients fight about money; if the family house was in a continual state of remodeling, the client's house is being remodeled; if the father couldn't keep a job, the client can't keep a job; if the family was evicted and moved frequently, the client moves frequently, etc.

The point to all this is for the client to become aware that he has been programmed for certain things in his youth and, as a result, uses this programming in his adult life. This is normal. This programming covers a broad range of life skills and attitudes: the parental values on education may affect whether one works with his hands or his "head." Parental demeanor may affect whether one speaks with authority or timidity, maintains eye contact or not, uses Oxford English or a southern drawl; family speech patterns and figures of speech are acquired. All of this is perfectly normal.

Once this normalcy is understood, one can begin detaching from any shame and guilt around these behaviors (especially acting out the financial scripts). It becomes clear we were taught that "2 + 2 = 5," that we learned the lesson well, and that is why so many things seem to be problems for us today. It also becomes clear that we can relearn a few simple facts and be on our way. In other words, although it may take years to clean up our financial messes, the right way of doing things can be learned and internalized in only a few short months. This has been particularly encouraging to my clients, for whom financial sanity is the proverbial light at the end of the recovery tunnel.

9

Clearing the Land

If you were going to build your own house you would need to follow a logical course of action. First you would need to survey and purchase a piece of land. After the survey is complete you are sure of what you "own" and don't own. Now you must remove anything that will get in the way of building your house. In the real world sense, this may include digging up boulders, cutting down trees, or bulldozing a hill. Or it may mean getting rid of some man-made problem, like a junked car or old refrigerator. Even if you've never built a house, you can see that it doesn't make sense to try to make something while there are obstacles in your way. Wouldn't it be strange to have a tree growing up through your living room or an old junkie car in your basement?

So what financial obstructions do you need to remove? Your debts! That's right, before you can build anything financially meaningful for yourself, you must be committed to eliminating debt from your life. The way to do this has two parts, much like the opposing blades on a scissors. One blade is abstinence from incurring debt, the other blade is a rational and systematic plan to pay off the debt we already have. Like the scissor blades, they must be used together to be effective. Together, they move us toward financial sobriety. (If you are currently debt-free, skip this section and go on to the next section; if not, stay here and suffer with the rest of us.)

Financial Sobriety As a Way of Life

One of the main mottos in Alcoholics Anonymous is that "It ain't a drinking problem, it's a thinking problem." Throughout the book, I've tried to make the point that financial dysfunctionalism is *not* a money problem. It is a defective view of and appreciation for oneself coupled with unworkable learned behavior. But there is, after all, this requirement to regain manageability of our finances.

It's impossible to continue to be an active alcoholic without using alcohol. It's impossible to be an active drug addict without using drugs. And it's impossible to be actively financially dysfunctional without using debt. That's right, the toxic substance of choice for financial self-abuse is debt—I have never encountered a client in my counseling practice who was on a "cash-only basis."

Financial Sobriety Is Zero Debt

For the alcoholic or addict who wishes to begin a life of sobriety, the very first step *must* be to quit using alcohol or drugs. Period. For the financially dysfunctional individual who wishes to begin a life of financial sobriety, he *must* begin with a commitment to quit using debt. Period. Not just credit cards and bank loans, but loans from family and friends, or paying for professional (or other services) "later." "Pay cash or do without" is the motto for financial recovery.

When I get to this point in my workshops or other presentations, howls of agony usually go up from the audience as the horrifying thought of life without credit cards and home mortgages begins to register. "How am I supposed to rent a car?" "I have to show a major credit card to cash a check at a store!" "If I don't use my credit, I'll lose my credit rating." Quit whining and keep reading.

Suppose, just suppose, that you awoke one day and read in the morning paper that the federal government had declared debt to be illegal . . . no credit cards, no car loans, no home mortgages, no school loans, no nothin'! Effective immediately. And the penalties for violations were severe. How would you go about living your life? What would change for you? What would your life be like five or ten years later?

Does it feel as though you'd be taking a pay cut to do without credit? Many people express feelings of great discomfort, even distress, as if they were being asked to reduce their income, when entering financial sobriety. Interesting, isn't it? In fact, debt by its very nature causes us to have less money (and therefore fewer, not more, things). For example, using a credit card having a 20 percent interest rate causes us to pay 20 percent more for our purchases than if we had paid cash. So, if we bought everything with credit cards, we'd have 20 percent less money available to spend because of the interest charges.

But wait . . . there's more! In his book, *Master Your Money* (Thomas Nelson Publishers, 1986), Ron Blue, an Atlanta CPA, makes an interesting point. He noted that the mere use of credit cards, whether paid off each month or not, will result in about 34 percent more purchases. That is, people who use credit cards, regardless of how quickly they pay down their balances, are likely to spend 34 percent more than those who do not use credit cards. Not only do credit cards make all our purchases cost more, but they statistically stimulate us to buy more! So what might happen if we just decided not to carry or use credit cards anymore? Hmm.

Maybe you think it would be difficult to cash a check without a credit card for identification. I can tell you that it's not impossible. When asked, I simply inform the clerk (with a certain disdain in my voice) that I don't use credit cards, and ninety-nine times out of one hundred my check is cashed anyway. Life goes on. In any event, every place I've been that would accept either a credit card or a personal check has always been willing to accept cash, too. What a remarkable system!

I must admit that I do things a little differently now than when I used credit cards. I used to wander through malls until I saw something interesting, and then I "charged" it on my credit card. Now, when I need something, I go out and look specifically for what I need, and shop for the best price. I do not purchase the item immediately, but think about the items I have seen and the price I must pay for what I want. After I have thought about it for a time, I go to the bank and withdraw the money needed from checking or from savings. Then I purchase the item, paying cash. I have the right amount with me for my purchase. I do not purchase any unplanned items (or they are very minimal, since I have only the cash for the purchase I had planned).

There is a reason for making the purchasing process so slow and deliberate: we, as adult children of dysfunctional families, were raised to meet our own needs as children, and the sooner, the better. This pattern of immediate gratification has become a way of life for us in all our affairs, including our financial affairs. As a result, we act impulsively and "medicate" reality by using debt to separate the pain of payment from the gratification of the purchase.

In slowing the process down, we are learning delayed gratification and it must be learned. By paying cash, we are no longer medicating financial reality. By paying cash or doing without, we are living in "the now." We are living in the reality that we have made other choices previously which exclude us from being able to enjoy the benefits of the purchase we may now be contemplating. Over a period of time, our choice-making will get better and better. We will give increasing thought to the long-term effects of our purchasing decisions. We will place increasing emphasis on value rather than mere convenience. We will begin to set priorities and plan ahead—to save! And it will get easier and easier, too, not just because we're practicing making better decisions, but because we will actually have more money available. This is because we are buying fewer things and making better choices about them. We are paying less for the purchases we make by choosing not to pay interest.

If I haven't already succeeded at getting you angry at debting in general, and your own debts specifically, I'll take another shot at it in the "Blueprinting" chapter that follows. In the end, I want you to be as abhorrent of debt as you are of alcohol, drugs, sugar, boundary-less relationships, or whatever your primary addiction or compulsion might be. I want your skin to crawl at the thought of using "other people's money."

Now that we have forged one blade of the scissors, the abstinence-from-debt blade, let us turn our attentions to the other blade, debt elimination.

Imagine that you are in a boat, several miles from shore. You notice there are several holes of different sizes in the bottom of your boat and water is coming in. Clearly, unless you stop the leaks, your boat will sink and you will drown. You also notice that you have the material to plug each hole and stop the leaking, but you must take action and move quickly. Doesn't it make sense that you would begin by plugging the biggest hole first, then the next biggest hole, and so on, until all the holes are plugged? And doesn't it make sense that no other plans you have will be as important as keeping your ship from sinking?

This life-and-death focus on plugging the leaks is the same approach that should be taken toward eliminating your debt. Your debts act just like the holes in the bottom of a boat and will, ultimately, sink you. Trust me. So, you want to retire the debt in a rational and systematic way. Just like plugging the holes, you want to stop the specific debt that is "sinking" you fastest. Here's how to do it:

1) Get a pencil, an eraser, a sheet of columnar accounting paper and a calculator.

2) On the columnar paper, list all your debts:
    a) Arrange them in descending interest rate order.

        i) Put those "no interest" loans from family and friends just ahead of your mortgage on this list.

        ii) Put income taxes in arrears at the top of the list.

    b) From left to right, record the interest rate, the payee, the regular payment and the balance due this month (before any payment)—round everything to whole dollars.

    c) Do *not* include ordinary living expenses, like the phone, electricity or groceries on this list (this is *not* a budget).

    d) *Do* put amounts you owe doctors, dentists and therapists on this list, even if they don't charge interest.

3) Add up the total payments
    a) If those personal loans don't have a required payment, enter zero in the payment column for each of them.

4) Add up the total of the balances due
    a) For some debts, like car loans, you may have to call the lender to get the balance owed. So call.

Your sheet should look something like the example at the end of the chapter. For many people, this listing will be the first clear, comprehensive picture of the situation they have seen. For many couples, this is often the first time one of the spouses is even aware of the existence of certain debts. This step is very similar to Step #8 of the 12-Steps of Alcoholics Anonymous: "Make a list of all persons we have harmed and become willing to make amends to them all." It's clear, honest and complete. The sense of relief and freedom that comes just from preparing this schedule is a reward in itself.

Of course, merely making a list is not going to propel us toward wholeness. We need action. Step #9 of the 12-Steps of Alcoholics Anonymous instructs us to "Make direct amends to such individuals . . . " In a similar vein, we now are ready to make financial "amends," i.e., to pay people what we owe them.

Committing suicide doesn't qualify as making amends. "Poor form" as our British friends might say. One thing we must consider at this point is whether we can actually live through, financially speaking, repayment of our debts. When we total our monthly debt payments, we must decide whether it is possible (not whether it is convenient or easy) to pay our creditors. Let's face it, 80 percent of the people who buy this book are probably facing a crisis owing to unmanageable debt; another 10 percent are buying it to give to someone else who needs to be "fixed," and the last 10 percent manage to have financial crises without debts (they're the ones skipping this section).

If it is impossible to repay your debt obligations and still survive, then continuing to try to make payments is going to be tantamount to financial suicide. It just won't work. If you suspect it is impossible for you, you have two options. Both will begin with getting a second opinion because, unfortunately, you can't trust your own judgment at this point in your financial recovery. That second opinion might be a trusted friend or your sponsor, if you are in a 12-Step program. Keep in mind that many of your friends are also likely to be just as financially dysfunctional as you are. The advice you seek should probably be limited to determining whether the current payments are possible or impossible for you.

Another alternative is to seek help from the Consumer Credit Counseling office near you. Generally, there is no charge for this help. CCC's people can help you in one of three ways:

1) They can help you develop a spending plan (actually a short-term budget) built around repaying your debts,

2) They can sometimes intercede for you in reducing (somewhat) your payments and/or the interest rate charged by creditors, and

3) They can tell you when you should choose "Option B," bankruptcy.

My belief is that all these skills (and several others) ought to be transferred to the client, but are usually not. In my practice, I teach my clients how to work up a spending plan, how to call and/or write to creditors to ask for help in working out payment arrangements, and how to make the decision for themselves about Option B. In the end, the client *must* own these skills or be doomed to repeating the behavior that led him to this problem in the first place. (Sample letters to creditors can be found at the end of this chapter.)

Bankruptcy

Let's talk about Option B. Bankruptcy is, in a manner of speaking, a last resort. It is a viable alternative, but one that I hope my clients can avoid. The reason for my hope is very simple and does not hinge on any moralistic belief: if a person comes from a toxic family of origin and carries with him toxic shame, it seems reasonable to me that bankruptcy is going to plug deeply into that shame core. The result may be that additional shame and guilt about "failing" or "robbing others" will produce yet another stigma to be endured or relieved through therapy. The greatest danger is that nothing else will be learned and, therefore, nothing else will change. The pressure gone, no incentive for change exists. I have yet to have a client continue counseling with me after filing bankruptcy.

If you have considered bankruptcy, there are five things you should know. First, it is a specialty area of law and you should seek only an attorney who is a qualified specialist to represent you.

Second, every bankruptcy attorney will want his fee to be paid in advance (which only makes sense). The fee will probably range upwards from $500, depending on the complexity of your case and the area of the country in which you live. Third, there are two types of bankruptcy. One eliminates all your unsecured debt (like credit cards and personal lines of credit). The other allows you to negotiate lower payments, longer payment times, and perhaps lower balances with creditors—all under court protection. Fourth, you don't lose everything you own nor can you discharge all your debts. Specifically, you cannot discharge any taxes you owe, nor student loans, nor certain secured debt (such as your home mortgage). Fifth, filing bankruptcy is like having a baby: it's painful, there is no privacy, and it's a matter of public record. And, unless your financial "promiscuity" is addressed, you're doomed to repeat this behavior.

Having made your list of indebtedness and confirmed that it really is possible for you to repay your creditors, get yourself out of debt as fast as possible. The first thing that occurs to most of my clients is to take out a consolidation loan or a second mortgage on their home. This approach appears to make sense mathematically (i.e., replacing high-interest, short-term debt with low-interest, long-term debt reduces payments and decreases the total interest paid). A second mortgage may look even more appealing when it has the "blessings" of the Government and your CPA because it's tax-deductible. Of course your banker will be very supportive and approving of your decision too—not that anyone in recovery really needs or seeks approval. It sure seems like the right thing, the responsible thing to do. *Don't do it!*

The reason it looks so right is that it's part of the same process, the same distorted, unworkable thinking, that led you to unmanageable debt in the first place. Notice what's taking place when you refinance your debt. First, you are reinforcing the idea that "debt fixes things," "debt makes my pain go away." Substitute the word "alcohol" for "debt" and see what you think. Switching from scotch to beer won't change the nature of alcoholism. Switching from credit card debt to second mortgage debt doesn't change anything either. That's the second point: nothing will have changed for you. The new loan, whether from a bank or friend or relative, will have simply rescued you. You'll have been enabled one more time. You may even go through some motions, like "taking the oath" and cutting up your credit cards, but that doesn't fool me. Maybe that superficial bullshit works on people outside recovery. It might even impress your therapist. But try it with your sponsor, if you are in a 12-Step program, and see what happens. I believe a second mortgage or consolidation loan is only valid when it becomes *the only alternative to bankruptcy*. Even then it's a toss-up.

So now we've eliminated bankruptcy and we've ruled out any sort of consolidation loan. At least we've agreed that bankruptcy or another loan will not change or fix anything. They'll merely provide relief from the symptoms, like aspirin works on a hangover. Let's figure out how to get rid of this obnoxious debt as fast as possible.

Imagine again that you are back in the boat, several miles from shore, plugging up the holes in the bottom to keep from sinking. After all the holes are repaired and you have bailed out all the water, your boat seems to float just fine. You are aware that while you were working on the leaks, the boat didn't move. You realize you didn't have time to plot a course for some other distant destination, either. You were totally committed to keeping the boat afloat.

This is exactly how to retire your debt. You have listed your debts on a sheet of paper in descending interest rate order. The interest rate, not the balance due or the payment amount, is the size of the "hole" in the bottom of your financial boat. Your debt extinguishment plan, then, will be to pay off the highest interest rate debt first, then the next highest interest rate, and so on. As in the boat analogy above, paying off your debt will consume all your attention and energy until you are no longer at risk of sinking. Forget about retirement. Forget about any other future financial plans. For now, your focus will be on paying off your debts. The interest you are paying is like the water pouring into the bottom of your boat. The interest you pay holds you back from realizing any other plans or dreams you might have.

Here's how to do it. First, round each payment amount upward to the nearest $5 (e.g., a payment of $73.26 would be rounded to $75). Next, total all the monthly payments you are required to make. This total will become the amount you will pay each month to get out of debt. Over time, as the balances on your credit card debts decline, you will notice that the minimum payments on each will be less. Ignore the billing statements and pay what is shown on your list. The total amount you pay your creditors will be the same each month.

Sooner or later, one of the creditors will be paid off. The rule is to pay the same total amount each month, so we must do something with the payment we were sending to this now-paid-off creditor. Going back to the boat analogy, we will now add this creditor's payment to the amount being paid to the creditor at the top of the list. As additional creditors are paid off, we will similarly add their payments to the payment being made to the creditor at the top of the list, always "patching the biggest hole first." Our total of payments never changes.

Besides getting out of debt the fastest way, two other things are happening. First, we have brought structure and stability to this area of our finances. I cannot overemphasize the importance of keeping constant the total repayment amount in this phase of your financial recovery. As in every other area of recovery, the acquisition of consistent behavior is crucial. Structure and stability are both items that have eluded us in our chaotic upbringing. And here we are actually practicing them. Second, we now have a plan for getting out of debt instead of just wishing and suffering. We are no longer passive victims of creditors or circumstances. We have (re)claimed certain personal power and are now proactive rather than reactive.

As enthusiastic as we may be starting out, we may tire of this process at some point. Remember that two of the common characteristics of adult children of dysfunctional families are "difficulty following a project through completion" and "fear of success." This debt retirement plan *will* succeed. It always has and it always will. Maybe it would be helpful if there were some way to maintain our enthusiasm over the long haul.

Anyone who has entered a weight loss program knows the first step before any session: you "weigh in." You get on the scales, weigh yourself, and write it on your chart. It's a reality check, pure and simple. You can't fool the scales with billowy clothing or large flower prints or bright colors. This checkpoint allows you to see your progress or, if you relapse, your problem.

We need a periodic "weigh in" for our debt problem too. On the worksheet where you listed your debts, you have columns out to the right, one column for each month. Here you will list the balance you still owe to each creditor in that month. Some creditors, like credit cards, send you a monthly statement from which you will simply copy down the balance owed. Don't do any math or adjust for payments you made. Just *copy* the balance onto your sheet. Other creditors, like for your mortgage and car loans, don't send statements. You'll have to call them and ask them for the balance for the month. It takes about sixty seconds to do that (you'll need your account number when you call), so don't even think about using the excuse that you didn't have time. When you have all the balances written in the column for this month, total them up. The total is your "Financial Flab Factor." If it helps you, just think of debt as excess body fat—useless, burdensome, and possibly life-threatening.

If you've ever tried to lose weight, you know that the first pound is a lot easier to lose than the last pound. But an interesting thing happens when we start shedding our financial flab: it's the other way around. More interest is paid early in the term of every loan, less at the end. Of course, the higher the interest rate of any loan, the more total interest will be paid. If you "pay ahead" on a loan, however, the excess over the required payment is applied to the principal (the amount you still owe). That reduces the amount on which the interest is calculated, so less of the next payment goes toward interest and more against the principal, and so on.

With our plan, we are ganging up on the highest interest rate debt first. We want to get rid of that "bad boy" as fast as possible. Even before we can make additional payments, the mere action of paying our debts according to plan will have the effect of reducing the total debt. So we total our balances due each month. We look at the difference in the totals from month to month. We notice that each month our total indebtedness is falling faster and faster. For example, you might notice that if January's total was $275 lower than December's total, February's total was $328 lower than January's, and March's was $392 lower than February's. From month to month, your debt will be melting away at an ever increasing rate as time goes on. It's really exciting to see progress coming faster and faster without any additional effort on your part!

It's important to keep this part exciting because this financial detoxification may take a long time. It's not unusual for this process to take several years. The time it takes is contingent on three things: how much you owe, how much you make, and how much you really want to be debt-free. I can't change how much you now owe or your current income, so perhaps I can motivate and encourage you.

Take just a moment for yourself right now. Think how peaceful and prosperous your life would be today if you didn't owe anybody *anything*. Imagine writing out checks to pay all your bills—at one sitting—and having money left over. Plenty of money. So much money that you regularly put some into your savings account. (You know, savings account . . . the other thing the bank has besides checking, VISA and the automatic teller?)

Notice that this exercise is founded on the concept that you are (or are becoming) debt-free. You are envisioning what your life will be like when you get to keep all the money you are now paying on debt. As your debts get smaller and smaller, your choices in life increase. Of course if one is heavily invested in remaining a victim, the absence of debt (bondage) is a frightening concept. It may be so frightening that the vision is actually "blocked" by our subconscious.

If you are having difficulty imagining this picture of yourself, do you see a problem? If you are unable to see yourself prospering, having money left over after paying the bills, or having a savings account, start with a smaller picture and work your way along. Perhaps you could first see yourself having enough money to pay all your bills and having just enough left to eat and do a few things. Next time, you could see yourself at the end of the month with an extra amount, like $10 or $20, in your checking account. Something unexpected would come along that you needed that money for, and you would be glad you had the money to pay for it. The next time you visualize your finances, you could see yourself with $10 left over every month (every payday?), then $15, and so on. Practice and repetition are important. Saying your visualization out loud is particularly powerful!

Our "clearing" away the obstacles is now complete. We have a regimen for paying off our debts in the fastest way possible, and we have connected that to giving ourselves permission to live a debt-free life. This permission is based on both a desire to abstain from debt, the toxic substance of choice for those of us who are financially dysfunctional, and a visualization of ourselves simply having more money in our lives as a result of being debt-free. Once we have undertaken these exercises, we are ready to begin our "blueprint" for prosperity. It is more difficult than what we have been working on up to this point, but it contains a unique feature that will help us stay focused on retiring our debts. In fact, the "blueprint" will make you very angry . . . some of the anger will be directed at your debts, and you may just find this to be very helpful. Onward, brothers and sisters.

DEBT ELIMINATION WORKSHEET

Balance Due from the Monthly Statement ----------

% A.P.R.	Creditor	Monthly Payment	(month)	(month)	(month)	(month)	(month)	(month)	(month)
____ %		$____	$____	$____	$____	$____	$____	$____	$____
	TOTALS	=====	=====	=====	=====	=====	=====	=====	=====

Using pencil, list all debts, in descending interest rate order rounding off to the next highest whole dollar amount. Pay the same total amount each month.

As debts are retired, apply those payments to the debt on the list with the highest interest rate.

Dear _____,

I am writing this letter because I need your help.

Presently I am experiencing financial difficulties and have sought professional assistance to resolve them. My CPA, Mr. George B. Moore, has suggested that I write immediately to notify you of my intentions and to enlist your support.

First, I want to acknowledge that I owe you $_____ as shown on my _____ statement.
(month)

Second, I want to assure you that it is my intention to pay you all all of the money I owe, including interest, and to avoid filing bankruptcy if at all possible.

Third, I want you to know that, together with Mr. Moore, I will be developing a plan within two weeks to repay you, and my other creditors, as quickly as possible; I will forward a copy of my plan to you on or before _____.
(date)

Fourth, I think it would be in both our interests if you would no longer extend credit to me . . . I intend to adopt a "cash only" spending policy. Thank you for your patience during this difficult time.

Sincerely,

Subject: Debt repayment plan

Dear Sir or Madam,

Recently I wrote to you about my financial difficulties and the fact that I was working with Mr. George B. Moore, CPA, to develop a workable repayment plan.

This letter outlines for you the plan we have developed and enlists your support and continued patience while I repay all my creditors.

Attached is a list of my creditors in descending interest rate order. Also shown are the balances due to each, as of their most recent statements, and the monthly payments I plan to make.

The plan calls for paying a fixed amount (the total of all monthly payments shown) each month. When a creditor has been paid in full, the amount normally paid to that creditor will be added to the payment on the open balance with the highest A.P.R. This process, which is designed to retire the most costly debt first, will be repeated until all creditors are paid in full.

I shall keep you informed both as to my progress and any problems which arise that would keep me from fulfilling my plan. I appreciate your continued cooperation in resolving this matter.

Sincerely,

10

Blueprinting—
Making Your Plan

Let's go back to our house-building analogy in the last chapter. If you were to have an architect design a house for you, he'd have to know two things: where you planned to build (i.e., the lay of the land) and how much you could afford to spend. Architects know that flat lots accommodate different designs than lots on hillsides, for example. Sometimes you can change what you have: you could bulldoze an uneven lot, and your architect would design a structure accordingly. Whether you are spending $50,000 or $500,000 makes a big difference in the size, features, and materials of the house. The architect needs to know what to expect before beginning the project.

Few people would engage a professional to design a $500,000 home in Arizona while having only $50,000 to spend and a lot located in Arkansas. That's because the reality is vastly different from the planning. Is it wrong to want a $500,000 home in Arizona (or the location of your choice)? No. Is it wrong to have $50,000 to spend and a lot in Arkansas? Certainly not. Wouldn't a lavish hacienda in Arizona be nicer than a tract home in Arkansas? Probably, but it doesn't really matter in this example, does it? The hacienda is merely a dream, a wish at this point, far removed from the facts of today. But if we have a dream, we can begin to develop plans to get there someday, and we can take action on those plans. Those are possibilities. But let's just stay in today for now.

Financial Reality

I can't tell you how many times I've seen people planning to build the big house in Dreamland when their resources and roots were elsewhere. It happens all the time. It happens to me. Time for a reality check before we start drawing up our plans.

Financial reality is what this chapter (indeed, this book) is all about. If you are truly financially dysfunctional, this chapter will be exceedingly stressful for you. Bummer! The good news is that the exercises in this chapter are exceptionally therapeutic.

Financial Reality #1 is: *Everything turns to junk.* That's right, junk! Think about it: everything you have ever owned has turned (or is turning) into junk. Everything you will ever own or hope to own will also turn into junk. Sooner or later it'll become just another landfill item, a curiosity perhaps for future generations of archaeologists. Junk, junk, junk.

How does that impact our planning? In two ways: first, we have to figure that everything will need to be replaced eventually (or we will have to live without it). That's something that lends itself to calculations and planning. Second, in the long run, it may change our perspective on just how important "things" are to us. However, changing our perspective would be a by-product of the planning process.

This brings us to Financial Reality #2: *There's no such thing as a "financial emergency"* . . . *we have to create them!* How do we do that? We simply pretend that everything we buy will last forever (another unnatural act) and keep buying more things. We save little or no money to replace or repair anything. When Financial Reality #1 (Everything turns to junk) hits us, we're surprised. We act as if this is the first pair of shoes, dishwasher, set of tires, or furnace that anyone has ever had to replace. Or we act like victims of a conspiracy of inanimate objects: Why couldn't the tires have lasted until spring? (They hate me!) Why did the furnace choose to go out now? (It's out to get me!) It becomes a financial emergency.

Maybe we feel that we must now choose between this emergency item and this weekend's entertainment. Or that we must choose between this item and our vacation or making the mortgage or rent payment. We must act quickly, choosing between few, and unpleasant, alternatives. What a crisis! What stress—remember? How do I get out of this thing? How can I get money quickly? I know—I'll borrow money . . . then it will be okay.

Which brings us to Financial Reality #3: *Using debt gets us less, not more; it just gives it to us sooner.* See the preceding chapter for a re-cap on this concept.

There's an old maxim that says something like, "If you don't know where you're going, don't complain when you get there." Today you have a choice: continue the pattern of passive self-abuse, having no financial direction (which has brought you to reading this book, for crying out loud) or plan for change. I assume you'd rather change (or at least explore change).

Starting the Financial Plan

Let's begin the planning process with a single, small step. You can easily understand that the shoes you are wearing right now will wear out eventually. Perhaps you will have them resoled and reheeled (like I do), but eventually they'll need to go. When you need new shoes, you'll go to the shoe store, try on a few pairs of shoes, select one pair, and pay for them. It isn't a big deal because you've had to replace shoes over and over during your entire life. God willing, you'll live a lot longer and buy more pairs of shoes in the future.

When you pay for the new pair of shoes, you probably think of it as "buying shoes." But since they, too, will wear out, it's as if you are really buying the right to wear these shoes for a while (maybe a year, maybe two). It's almost like we rent our shoes, isn't it? We just pay all the rent up front (prepaid rent, as the accountants say).

If we knew about how long the shoes would last, we could calculate the "monthly rental", couldn't we? Let's see, if the shoes cost $48 and lasted one year (12 months), the "monthly rental" would be $48/12 months = $4/month. In this example, it costs us $4 per month to wear shoes. Maybe your shoes cost more or less and maybe yours wear out sooner or later than one year. But you can do the math and figure it out.

If a dishwasher costs $600 (including installation and taxes), and it lasts for ten years (120 months), then the "monthly rent" is $600/120 months = $5/month. We don't know exactly when it will wear out, but we *do* know that it will wear out. If we set aside $5 each month, when (not *if*) it wears out, we will have set aside enough to pay for the next dishwasher. In cash!

So a person who wears $48 shoes for one year and who owns a $600 dishwasher for ten years needs to set aside $9 per month ($4 for shoes plus $5 for the dishwasher) to pay the rent on these two items. In that way, that person will always have a pair of shoes and a dishwasher and will always be able to pay cash for them.

What Does It Really Cost to Live?

But what about the person who wants more out of life than just a pair of shoes and a dishwasher? What about socks and dishes? I'm glad you asked. We can find out two things about anything we want to own: how much it would cost to buy (or replace) and about how long we can expect it to last. If we know these two things, we can calculate the monthly rent we have to pay to use any item. The total of all our monthly rents is what it really costs us to live.

Developing a What Does It Really Cost to Live worksheet is done in two phases. As with all worksheets, use a pencil and round everything to whole dollars. Phase One is the fact-finding part. It's time-consuming, but easy. Phase Two is quick, but can be very painful. Most people spend about thirty to forty five minutes a day for a month or so completing this project.

If you are married or in another exclusive relationship, it is imperative that both partners work on this project together, all the way to the end. Because of the stress that surrounds this effort, I suggest that each session be limited (fifteen to twenty-five minutes). Agree before you start as to how long the break will be between sessions. Set the oven timer, and when the bell rings, drop your pencils, drop the subject (i.e., shut up), and take a walk in separate directions. Be aware that during the work, it will be the nine-year-old financial inner child in each of you who is present. Two nine-year-olds can't work on anything for very long without fighting. Neither will you. You needn't suppress it, just be aware of it.

For couples, the What Does It Really Cost to Live worksheet will be a negotiated settlement. That means that each person will be equally disgusted with the outcome. (If you are single, you'll have to be disgusted all by yourself.) If one person is a "winner," then this blueprint calls for building on a fault. In the end, the financial house will fail.

Phase One—Get the Facts

First, make a detailed list of all the things you own, want to own, or expect to do in life. Look at the example at the end of this chapter to see how to do this.

Second, find out exactly how much each of these items costs (i.e., amount you will have to write the check for, including sales taxes, installation, etc.). Get actual, hard-nosed facts. Note that I just made up all the numbers used in the example, so don't use any of them for your worksheet. Couples can split up the fact-finding jobs. Men generally like to handle gathering facts on mechanical items like cars, dishwashers, downspouts, etc. Women generally prefer to work with quality-of-life items like furniture, vacations, clothing, etc. You choose. You can look in catalogs or shop at stores to gather the facts. You can also phone people. It makes sense to call a heating contractor to get information about replacing your furnace, rather than to waste someone's time coming to your home when there's nothing wrong with your furnace.

Third, determine how many months will pass before you have to write another check for this same item. Often, experienced sales people can give you answers about longevity of a product. If not, consumer magazines and friends who have something similar can give you guidance.

Fourth, divide the cost of each item by the number of months the item will last (or until you have to pay for it) to determine the monthly rent.

Be sure to include the total debt and the combined monthly payments as a line item on your worksheet. This should be a "copy job" from the Debt Elimination worksheet you prepared in the previous chapter. If your Debt Elimination worksheet includes a mortgage loan(s) on your home, you'll want to be certain that you enter it only once on the What Does It Really Cost to Live worksheet. Either include it with the rest of the debts or put it on a line by itself with the rest of the housing expenses. I suggest you list your debt on the last line of the last page of the What Does It Really Cost to Live worksheet. That way, later, you will be able to direct some very healthy anger at Debt. Rrr!

There are three items on the What Does It Really Cost to Live worksheet which seem to be more difficult than the others for most people: gifts, children's college tuition, and vacations. I'd like to offer some helpful suggestions about them because I want you to succeed with this project and because it might help shape your thinking about these items in a healthy way.

Gifts

On a separate sheet of paper, down the left hand side list the names of all the individuals to whom you expect to be giving gifts this year. Add a couple of names at the bottom to account for the unexpected (e.g., "Unexpected #1", "Unexpected #2"). Across the top of the page, from left to right, name the various occasions on which you give gifts (e.g., Christmas, Hanukkah, Birthday, Anniversary, Shower, Graduation, Bar/Bat Mitzvah, etc.). Going down each occasion column, determine how much is reasonable to spend for each named individual and write the amount in that column across from his or her name. Continue the process until all occasions and names are accounted for.

Total all the numbers written on the page, and that will become the number you will write down on your What Does It Really Cost to Live worksheet in the Amount column. In the Number of Months column, you will write down "12." This is because you will want to set aside money for all these gifts at a regular rate, even though shopping in December may account for more than half your gift spending. For now, just trust me.

Speaking of shopping in December, I feel that additional encouragement and coaching is needed here. You may think that the finest minds in the country are working in hospital operating rooms and in the space program. I suspect that the best and the brightest are actually working in the advertising industry. Perhaps you have heard or read reports of how many retail stores make their entire yearly profits between Thanksgiving and Christmas. And perhaps you have felt an enormous pressure or gnawing dissatisfaction with yourself/your situation during this time of the year. I don't think that's a coincidence. Just as werewolves come out at the full moon, these great national talents are brought to full force every autumn. Those of us from toxic families have ample opportunities to feel "less than," shamed, different, and guilty. We are susceptible to forming financially inappropriate and unworkable expectations about Christmas. As a result, we are particularly prone to over-spending and then recycling the holiday spending stress when the bills come due in February. (March is one of the busiest months in my practice.)

May I suggest a different approach to Christmas shopping? I have found this technique to be very powerful and practically infallible. Before you go out shopping, get out your gift sheet to see how much you have planned to spend. Next, get a regular mailing envelope for each person on your list—write on the outside of each envelope the person's name. Place inside each envelope the amount of cash you have planned to spend for the person named. From your wallet or purse, remove your driver's license and put it in your pocket. Armed with only your envelopes and your driver's license (no checkbook, no credit cards, no extra cash), you are now ready to go shopping.

At the store, when you find the perfect gift for your good friend Mary, but it happens to be just a little more than you had planned on spending, you will see your choices clearly. Either you find something less expensive for her, or you take money from somebody else's envelope to buy her gift. The envelopes do *not* get replenished just because you took money from one for another.

This works in reverse as well. If you spend less for someone than you thought you would, you can choose to put that money into someone else's envelope or you can keep it! Radical concept, isn't it? You don't have to spend it!

This plan works because it's simple. It sets you up for success. Unless you choose to derail it, you will find that whatever spiritual meaning you attach to the December holidays can be detached from financial crisis and stress. If you don't like the tranquility and serenity, you can always go back to the old ways next year.

Children's College Tuition

Planning for your child's college expenses is another place where a lot of heartstrings get pulled. And, for the shame-based parent, this is yet another opportunity to feel failure. If we are stress-addicted, we will probably wait until our child is going through high school commencement exercises before we start planning to pay for college—maximum jolt. Sorta like the tires on the car—"Oh, sure, you would pick *now* to go to college."

In the process of developing your plan, many things will become clear to you. One of these will be that you, like most parents, may not be able to finance the entire cost of your child's college education, especially if you try to use the frightening statistics used by insurance agents, stockbrokers and others with personal agendas for your money. (You know, "The cost of educating a child born today at a four-year state university will be $1.4 billion . . . how will you come up with that?")

The fact is that you don't have to pay for your child's college education. The only person requiring you to do that is yourself. Sure, it would be nice to be able to do that, but if your child really wants a college education, he or she will get it. And if the desire isn't there, better to save your money for something that will make you happier than paying a lot of money for a four-year babysitting experience.

Perhaps you fit somewhere between not being able to provide all the money and not wanting to provide any money for the little ingrate(s). If assisting your child financially is a high priority for you, we still need some sort of rational plan. Here it is:

First, for each child you expect to be helping through, figure out how many months there are between now and his or her college graduation. We're not interested in when your child starts college because you don't need to have all the money then. You do need to have funds by the beginning of each year, semester, or however the college handles special payment plans (following the principle of pay cash or do without). This also gives you another four or five years to fund your assistance.

Again, using a separate piece of paper, write down each child's name. Next to each name write down the amount of money you hope to be able to provide for college (for example, $8,000 per child). Divide the amount by the number of months remaining till college graduation to get the amount you must set aside each month for each child. Add up the monthly amounts and put the total on your What Does It Really Cost to Live worksheet.

It may turn out that you are unable to afford the amount you had originally expected to set aside. In that case you will have to change the amount, divide by the months, and come up with a new monthly set figure. It doesn't mean that you're a failure or a bad person. It means you have a realistic sense of what you can (and will) do. It means your children will have a clear picture for school choices and what they will have to contribute to their own education. It means you have done a good job of giving everyone involved advance warning such that another "financial emergency" can be avoided! Congratulations!

Vacations

Vacations are great opportunities to create stress and to set up fun avoidance in our lives. (If we have such a lousy time on vacations, let's don't go any more often than we have to). For the stress-addicted vacationer, planning to take a vacation at the last minute or on impulse is a great way to get a "fix." Last-minute decisions virtually preclude any financial preparation, so the vacation money has to come out of something else—like the rent money or the grocery money—which sets up another round of crises. We really do create the financial crises in our lives.

To remove this stress from our lives is simple. On a separate piece of paper, write down where you plan to go on vacation. If you plan more than one getaway, write each on a separate piece of paper. Write down the date(s) of each vacation you envision. Have a calendar in front of you while you do this.

Think about when you will leave on your vacation and when you will return. How will you be transporting yourself? Will you be flying or driving? Write down how much that will cost. If you are driving, what will meals and lodging cost along the way? Write that down. If you will be staying in a hotel, write down how much that will cost for each day. Use real facts—call the hotel or a travel agent or get a brochure from AAA (American Automobile Association) to find out costs. How many meals will you be eating out? Remember that it's probably double what it costs to eat out "back home." Remember the tips. Write it down. What sort of entertainment will you be allowing yourself along the way and at the destination—ski lifts, museums, charter boat, theater, tours? Find out what it costs and write it down. You get the idea: think about the vacation from beginning to end, day by day, break the costs down by activity and write down the actual costs. When you have obtained all the facts about what you will be spending, add up all the costs (for each vacation). Divide the total by 12 months and record the results on you What Does It Really Cost to Live worksheet.

You've probably figured out that any other item on your worksheet (clothing, furniture, etc.) can be handled the same way. Break anything complex down into its components, determine the cost of each, add the costs and divide by the time period. Use separate sheets for each. In the interest of your sanity, use pencil, because now comes the painful part. *You will be doing a lot of erasing!*

Phase Two—Get the Axe

In Phase One, you gathered facts—how much something costs, how long it will last, and how much it breaks down to each month. You have recorded everything that you have (or envision having) in your life. If you have done it carefully, if you have gotten hard-nosed facts, you have invested a lot of time in this project and you now have the basis for some powerful therapy.

Phase Two begins with totaling the monthly amounts column on your What Does It Really Cost to Live worksheet. The total of all your monthly amounts is what it really costs to live the life you have depicted for yourself on the worksheet. In order to live this life, your total must be less than your after-tax income. Most of my clients find that the real cost of their lives exceeds their income by at least 30 percent, some up to 100 percent. Perhaps you've noticed a similar problem. (Who me?!)

After the initial shock from realizing that you can't possibly afford to live the life you've been trying to live, you may feel anger and despair. Many people who get this far get very angry at me, which is okay. My only rule is no hurting the messenger. Despair and a sense of hopelessness often wash over us at this point. All of these feelings (and probably some others that I don't even know about) are legitimate and normal. Feel the feelings, but trust that I didn't bring you this far to leave you here. I have a plan for change. And the pain you're feeling is necessary for the following "therapy" to be effective.

Since (or if) the cost of your lifestyle exceeds your current income, you'll need to put some items "back on the shelf." Go back over your worksheet and figure out which items will have to be eliminated or changed for now. Eliminating something now doesn't mean that you will never have it. It simply means that right now there isn't enough money coming into your life to buy certain items.

On paper and in your mind, you are developing a financial reality for yourself. You will notice that grocery coupons, less entertainment, or giving up cable TV alone will not make a significant difference (except perhaps to fulfill our "don't deserve" or "martyr" agendas). You are seeing that structural changes are required for your financial serenity. Perhaps you will have to drive your cars longer or buy cheaper, maybe used, cars. Perhaps you'll have to do all of the above. Maybe you can't really afford to live in the house you have right now. Many of my clients find that downsizing or selling their homes and renting is their only option for now. Maybe you can't finance $8,000 for each child's college education, but only $2,500. It's all okay because it's all real!

Phase Two is complete when the total of your monthly rents is less than your monthly income. I can't give you a lot of guidance on this part, since everyone has different value systems and priorities. You'll have to work it out the best way you can. Something that has helped me is reading Richard J. Foster's marvelous book, *Freedom of Simplicity* (Harper & Row). Foster's masterfully written book on clarifying personal values and material needs is presented from a Christian perspective, but I believe it can help anyone regardless of spiritual orientation.

As you work through this very stressful exercise, notice how your thinking about the amount of money you can spend on which items is being shaped. It will become very clear to you that if a VCR is not on the final list, you will *not* be buying a VCR (or a boat, shop tools, golf clubs, jewelry, new wardrobes, or anything else not on your worksheet).

You will have emerged from this process with a clear understanding of your complete financial picture, and how each expenditure is part of a delicately balanced whole. Changes are allowed, but new priorities mean that something else has to be given up. An unplanned purchase will throw the whole out of balance. Chaos and stress will follow. You have come too far to allow that! You are now financially centered and focused. You don't even need a budget (although you will want to check actual expenditures against your worksheet from time to time and adjust accordingly).

In the short term, taking things off the list is the only way to head off certain financial disaster. However, as we grow healthier in recovery, financially and otherwise, we may become aware of ways we have been blocking or thwarting income. Or we may not become aware of them, but simply notice that our income seems to increase without any conscious effort on our part to make that happen. As income begins to enter our lives in increasing amounts, we will be able to add back to our worksheet some of the things we had to eliminate earlier. The equilibrium is maintained because the expenditures each month still don't exceed our net income.

Phase Three—Implementation

Once we have determined which items on the list can stay in our lives, the final piece can be put in place. This is the implementation of the What Does It Really Cost to Live worksheet. It's probably the easiest part. In the example sheets shown, you'll notice two columns at the far right: Checking and Savings. Those items that are paid on a monthly basis should have that amount of money put directly into the checking account each month. Those items that are not paid monthly should be put into savings. A regular passbook savings account will do just fine. When one of the planned, non-monthly items must be paid for, simply transfer the money needed from savings to checking and pay cash for it.

An interesting phenomenon occurs upon implementing your worksheet: after about nine to twelve months, you will no longer experience financial emergencies. I'll spare you a mathematical explanation, but it's similar to the way an insurance company works. Each of the items on your worksheet has a known cost and a known life, you just don't know *when* it's going to go. So, if you're saving up for a large number of different items, the probability of all (or many) of them failing at the same time is very unlikely. When one item fails, because you are saving for many, you will have the money available to pay cash for it. Because you continue funding the item, even after you have just replaced it, when another item fails, you will have the money for it. And so on. I think it's really amazing.

The worksheet ultimately becomes your financial blueprint. The process of developing this blueprint has proven to be enormously therapeutic for those who have given it 100 percent. Couples who work through this together find two things: first, they have learned how to communicate about money, and second, there is enormous power in being in agreement on their finances. Everyone, whether single or married, finds improved clarity of thinking about resources and priorities to be one of the outcomes. Just imagine all the energy and time you expend worrying about your finances being directed into other, fun, areas of living. Wow!

What Does it Really Cost to Live?

INSTRUCTIONS: 1) Use pencil only,
                 2) Use whole $s only,
                 3) Work for short periods only,
                 4) STOP when total for Col. 3 is LESS THAN your after-tax income
Numbers shown here are fictitous and are used only to demonstrate how the worksheet is to be
used. A blank worksheet for you to use immediately follows.

HOME EXPENSES

EXPENSES	Probable $ Amt. to be paid	Paid every ??? mos.	Total required per month	Per mo. payments to checking	All other payments to savings
Mortgage or Rent	550	1	550	550	0
Property Taxes	247	6	41	0	41
Homeowners/Renters Ins.	135	12	11	0	11

Utilities

Gas	56	1	56	56	0
Electricity	85	1	85	85	0
Water/Sewage	112	3	37	0	37
Telephone	48	1	48	48	0

Major Replacements:

Furnace/Air Conditioner	3,875	180	22	0	22
Water Heater	655	120	5	0	5
Dishwasher	688	96	7	0	7
Clothes Washer	575	120	5	0	5
Clothes Dryer	454	120	4	0	4
Refrigerator	986	96	10	0	10
Oven/Stove/Range	823	120	7	0	7
Microwave Oven	350	96	4	0	4
Garbage Disposal	250	72	3	0	3
Roof	2,966	120	25	0	25
Gutters/Downspouts	483	60	8	0	8
Dehumidifier	257	60	4	0	4
Carpeting	3,569	120	30	0	30
Drapes/Window Treatments	1,839	72	26	0	26

Maintenance & cleaning:

Landscaping	1,200	12	100	0	100
Lawn Service	600	12	50	0	50
Snow Removal	250	12	21	0	21
Trash Removal	35	1	35	35	0
Gutter Cleaning	125	12	10	0	10
Painting	1,650	36	46	0	46
Housecleaning	96	1	96	96	0
Driveway Seal/Resurface	454	48	9	0	9
Windows	2,500	240	10	0	10
Draperies	1,500	144	10	0	10
Carpet Cleaning	60	6	10	0	10

Furniture & Accessories

Living Room	4,900	120	41	0	41
Dining Room	3,600	240	15	0	15
Bedroom #1	2,875	180	16	0	16
Bedroom #2	1,600	120	13	0	13
Bedroom #3	1,600	96	17	0	17
Kitchen	1,500	60	25	0	25
Family Room	1,500	60	25	0	25
Cookware, China, Towels, Linen	500	12	42	0	42

PERSONAL EXPENSES
Education:

Continuing/Professional	360	12	30	0	30
Degree Program	850	12	71	0	71
Children's Tuition	4,800	12	400	0	400
Children's College	20,000	120	167	0	167

Insurance:

Life	350	12	29	0	29
Hospitalization	420	1	420	420	0
Disability	480	12	40	0	40

Medical:

Medical Deductible	1,000	12	83	0	83
Dental	300	12	25	0	25
Optometry (Glasses, Contacts)	600	12	50	0	50
Hearing Aids, etc.	50	12	4	0	4
Prescriptions	125	12	10	0	10
Veterinarian	160	12	13	0	13

Clothing, shoes, accessories:

Work	1,200	12	100	0	100
Informal/Sports/Casual	1,500	12	125	0	125
Formal	600	12	50	0	50
Special Use (Skiing, etc.)	750	12	63	0	63
Children's	1,200	12	100	0	100
Dry Cleaning & Laundry	35	1	35	35	0

Other:

Charitable Contributions	5,200	12	433	0	433
Therapy	300	1	300	300	0
Vacations	2,400	12	200	0	200
Gifts	2,250	12	188	0	188

Food and Entertainment:

Groceries	400	1	400	400	0
Grooming/Toiletries	100	1	100	100	0
Meals Eaten Out	60	1	60	60	0
Entertainment (not Meals)	75	1	75	75	0
Dues, Subscriptions,	350	12	29	0	29
Cable TV	28	1	28	28	0

Automobile:

Cost of next Car/Truck	16,000	96	167	0	167
License Plates	48	12	4	0	4
Insurance	467	12	39	0	39
Fuel	80	1	80	80	0

Parking	75	1	75	75	0
Oil Changes	30	3	10	0	10
Tune-ups	90	6	15	0	15
Antifreeze	35	12	3	0	3
Air Conditioner	60	12	5	0	5
Tires	480	48	10	0	10
Brakes	129	48	3	0	3
Exhaust System	258	36	7	0	7
Repairs/Replacements	260	12	22	0	22

Automobile #2:

Cost of next Car/Truck	22,000	60	367	0	367
License Plates	48	12	4	0	4
Insurance	540	12	45	0	45
Fuel	120	1	120	120	0
Parking	5	1	5	5	0
Oil Changes	30	3	10	0	10
Tune-ups	180	9	20	0	20
Antifreeze	45	12	4	0	4
Air Conditioner	125	12	10	0	10
Tires	600	36	17	0	17
Brakes	350	36	10	0	10
Exhaust System	460	36	13	0	13
Repairs/Replacements	380	12	32	0	32

Retirement & related:

IRA/SEP	1,500	12	125	0	125
401 (k)	200	1	200	200	0
403 (b)			0	0	0
Union Dues	240	12	20	0	20
State Teachers Retirement			0	0	0
Other Savings/Investments	200	1	200	200	0
DEBTS (excl. mortgage):	**16,000**	**60**	**267**	**267**	**0**

TOTAL (must be less than after-tax income):   7,115   3,235   3,880

What Does it Really Cost to Live?

INSTRUCTIONS: 1) Use pencil only,
                   2) Use whole $s only,
                   3) Work for short periods only,
                   4) STOP when total for Column 3 is LESS THAN your after-tax income

HOME EXPENSES

EXPENSES	Probable $ Amt. to be paid	Paid every ??? per month	Total required per month	Per mo. pay- ments to checking	All other payments to savings
Mortgage or Rent					
Property Taxes					
Homeowners/Renters Insurance					

Utilities:

Gas					
Electricity					
Water/Sewage					
Telephone					

Major Replacements:

Furnace/Air Conditioner					
Water Heater					
Dishwasher					
Clothes Washer					
Clothes Dryer					
Refrigerator					
Oven/Stove/Range					
Microwave Oven					
Garbage Disposal					
Roof					
Gutters/Downspout					
Dehumidifier					
Carpeting					
Drapes/Window Treatments					

Maintenance & cleaning:

Landscaping					
Lawn Service					
Snow Removal					
Trash Removal					
Gutter Cleaning					
Painting					
House Cleaning					
Driveway Seal/Resurface					
Windows					
Draperies					
Carpet Cleaning					

Furniture & Accessories

Living Room					
Dining Room					
Bedroom #1					
Bedroom #2					
Bedroom #3					
Kitchen					
Family Room					
Cookware, China, Towels, Linen					

PERSONAL EXPENSES
Education:

Continuing/Professional					
Degree Program					
Children's Tuition					
Children's College					

Insurance:

Life					
Hospitalization					
Disability					

Medical:

Medical Deductible					
Dental					
Optometry (Glasses, Contacts)					
Hearing Aids, etc.					
Prescriptions					
Veterinarian					

Clothing, shoes, accessories:

Work					
Informal/Sports/Casual					
Formal					
Special Use (Skiing, etc.)					
Children's					
Dry Cleaning & Laundry					

Other:

Charitable Contributions					
Therapy					
Vacations					
Gifts					

Food and Entertainment

Groceries					
Grooming/Toiletries					
Meals Eaten Out					
Entertainment (not Meals)					
Dues, Subscriptions, Memberships					
Cable TV					

Automobile:

Cost of next Car/Truck					
License Plates					
Insurance					
Fuel					

Parking					
Oil Changes					
Tune-ups					
Antifreeze					
Air Conditioner					
Tires					
Brakes					
Exhaust System					
Repairs/Replacements					

Automobile #2

Cost of next Car/Truck					
License Plates					
Insurance					
Fuel					
Parking					
Oil Changes					
Tune-ups					
Antifreeze					
Air Conditioner					
Tires					
Brakes					
Exhaust System					
Repairs/Replacements					

Retirement & related:

IRA/SEP					
401 (k)					
403 (b)					
Union Dues					
State Teachers Retirement					
Other Savings/Investments					
DEBTS (excl. mortgage):					

TOTAL (must be less than after-tax income):

Part Three

New Spiritual Tools

11

Nailing It All Together

In Part One, I talked about the impact the family-of-origin experience plays in the formation of our adult beliefs and behaviors as they relate to money. The main purpose of that discussion was to help the financially dysfunctional reader detach from the shame and guilt of having "money problems." We also learned that money problems don't have anything to do with money, per se. Income Avoiding and Over-spending roles were exposed so that you could examine your behavior without secrecy or shame, and change it if you wanted to.

Part Two was concerned with the "nuts and bolts" of regaining financial manageability. Thus far, we have focused on the monetary aspects only. This may lead you to think that the monetary aspects are the most important part of the process, but that isn't true. The reason for the presentation sequence is that most people want to jump into "fixing the money part" as soon as possible. In my opinion, the most important part of the whole book is what follows.

Part Three deals with the spiritual (or intangible) side of financial recovery. This is where all the power truly resides. In order to have spiritual growth, a spiritual healing, we must separate ourselves from the non-spiritual. That is, we must be able to differentiate between our spiritual self and our non-spiritual self. My belief is that our spiritual self is inside of us trying to get out rather than being outside of us trying to get in. Often, difficulty with allowing our spirituality to emerge is rooted in painful experiences with a particular clergyperson, congregation or religious denomination. Sometimes the problem is with an overcontrolling parent and has been generalized to any authority figure, including God or his "policemen:" the priests, nuns, etc. Frequently, people who have diminished spirituality have allowed themselves to be turned off by "religious" people who are obnoxiously overzealous, dull, hypocritical or all of the above. In short, external events or circumstances have once again been internalized by our child self. Would I want to be "adopted" by a parent who has kids like them? No way!

Earnie Larsen, my hero, has a great line on one of his many fine tapes that says, "God is not your father in a God-mask." At the time I first heard that, I had thought my relationship with God was quite good. However, Earnie's statement showed me that I still attributed many characteristics to God that I had seen in my father. Those characteristics kept me from getting close, trusting Him, and, therefore, trusting anyone else. Today the God of my understanding is gentle, loving, and kind. He is infinitely patient, allowing me to make numerous mistakes (or the same mistake numerous times). He is protective, letting me experience the consequences of my actions without suffering permanent harm. And He is generous, seeing that all my needs are met, whether I deserve it or not. My God loves me just the way I am and has a special purpose for me and my life. I don't always understand His plan, but I know it exists. I don't always understand my part, but when I listen, I hear the instructions. I don't always get it right the first time, but I get as many chances as I need.

Whether your spiritual values and your God-concept are the same as mine is not important. All that is important is that you be open to change. Not all change is good, however, so we need to constantly test the changes in us to be sure we're headed in the right direction.

God has placed in my awareness some spiritual exercises which I have used with great success. I have shared these exercises with other clients in my practice. Their results have often been astounding to them and to me. In keeping with the tone of the rest of this book, everything I will give you is concrete, fully tested and idiot-proof. The *only* way to fail with any of these exercises is to avoid doing them! Having said all that, let's get started.

Financial Gargoyles

This exercise is painful, fun, and extremely powerful! Perhaps you already know what a "gargoyle" is. If you don't, a gargoyle is one of those hideous stone monsters carved on the parapets of medieval cathedrals. Pagan stonecarvers placed them all around the churches to ward off evil spirits. As the masons were also practical men, the gargoyles often served as downspouts. Rainwater from the church roof would spew from the gargoyles open mouths so that it wouldn't run down the stone walls, washing them away.

From a distance, when one looks at the cathedrals, the gargoyles don't stand out. They are just part of the architecture. They have been there for hundreds of years and will be for hundreds more. Although the gargoyles seem to have a function, they are ugly and spiritually contrary to the teachings of the church. No one building a church today would put gargoyles on it. But still the ancient creatures stand.

In your life, you have financial gargoyles. Ugly things whose usefulness has long since passed. Things which are spiritually contrary to healthy beliefs. Things which are keeping you stuck without your even knowing it!

If you are having difficulty envisioning what these could possibly be for you, some examples might help. Imagine yourself in your bedroom, standing in front of your dresser. See yourself opening the drawer containing your underwear. As you look down into the drawer, you are aware that there is something down at the bottom or off to the back which is ugly. Maybe it's a pair of underpants with holes or stains or elastic that doesn't stretch anymore. It's something that you'd be embarrassed to be wearing if you had to be taken to the hospital, isn't it? You'd probably be ashamed if your neighbor even saw you waxing your car with it. That item is a gargoyle.

Now go to your sock drawer. See that sock which lost its mate long ago? See the socks that have faded or shrunk or whose color just doesn't seem to go with anything? See the sock(s) with the holes in the toes or in the heels? When was the last time you wore any of them? Gargoyles!

In your closet, way over to the side (or in the back) are some clothes that you wore when you were thinner. They hang there now, silently mocking you, saying, "Boy, you really got fat, didn't you? Remember how nice you looked when you wore me? And look at me . . . you only wore me once! What a waste of money! You are irresponsible with your body, your money, and your life." Gargoyles!

Or maybe the clothes which are pushed aside are from a time when you were heavier. They mock you, saying, "Sure you're thin now. But you don't have the willpower to stay thin. You'll be back sooner or later. We're waiting for you to gain all that weight back. We know this thin stuff is just temporary for you." Gargoyles!

At the bottom of the closet is a pair of shoes which hasn't been worn in a long time. They're covered with a fine patina of dust. The insides are all dried up and the leather is curled and brittle. Maybe the heels are round and the soles are worn through. You know the ones I mean. Gargoyles!

Other gargoyles include the lamp with the short-circuit or the broken shade, the TV that doesn't work, the wedding gift you can't stand (or only put out when the giver comes to town), and the toaster that always burns your toast. The books or magazines you haven't looked at in umpteen years, the towel that is frayed and so worn you can see through it, the broken things you've been meaning to fix someday (but never seem to have the time for), the ballpoint pen that has long since dried up, the utility bills from 1983, Christmas gift receipts from two years ago—all are gargoyles. Get the picture?

The message these items have in common is that this is all you deserve. "You only deserve to be surrounded by broken, defective, useless things because that's what you are," they seem to shout. And they are shouting at you twenty-four hours a day. They don't even take holidays off. Silencing them seems to be an obvious course of action.

Here's how to do it. Each day for forty consecutive days select one (and only one) of your gargoyles and throw it out of your life. Notice the instructions have three distinct parts: first, it's one item each day; second, it's done for forty consecutive days; third, it must by *yours* (not your spouse's or child's). The instructions seem fairly simple to me, but often clients have tried to make something complex out of the exercise. Allow me to anticipate some questions you may have. No, having a garage sale is not the same thing. No, selling an item is not the same thing. No, giving it to your sister, brother, father, mother, or friend is not the same thing (that simply makes them the curator of your Museum of Horrors). No, cleaning out the attic, garage, or basement is not the same thing. Yes, you can count a drawer or a box as a single item.

If it's junk, put it in the garbage. If it's an article of clothing you can no longer use and it's in nice condition, give it to the church, Goodwill, or Salvation Army. Don't give junky clothes to the poor; they have enough problems without taking on your rags. Rags go in the rag bag or in the trash.

It is important that you toss only one item each day for forty days. Here's why: any behavior that you repeat for forty consecutive days becomes a habit. This doesn't mean that you will become compulsive about pitching out everything you own. It means that your tolerance for gargoyles (and your ability to recognize them) will be permanently altered. Obviously, cleaning out the attic (or garage or basement) is another "all or nothing" grand effort, not sustainable for forty days and, therefore, not life-changing. Large cleaning projects also deny you the opportunity to come into conscious contact with the gargoyles.

Conscious contact with each of these is extremely important to the success of this exercise. This is because each item we terminate has a whole host of memories and beliefs that we have associated with it. By focusing on it, really thinking about it, we bring those memories and beliefs up to our awareness in a way that wholesale cleaning does not allow. As we terminate the thing, we are also releasing the memories and beliefs about it. That's one of the major components toward healthier thinking contained in this exercise. This process, done for forty consecutive days, also becomes permanent.

Clients often report anxiety about letting go of their gargoyles until they actually dump them. But immediately afterward, they experience great relief, even pleasure. After undertaking this exercise, clients have reported significant changes in how they feel overall, and specifically how they feel about themselves. Some note changes after only a few days, others after a longer period.

Isn't it interesting that psychotherapy is largely about getting rid of emotional baggage, psychological "junk," with the result that the client feels better? Here we are getting rid of tangible junk and feeling better afterward. Permanently! And it doesn't cost us anything to do it! (Note: I'm not suggesting that this exercise is a substitute for therapy, but I do believe it can significantly accelerate or enhance total recovery.)

Take a moment now to reflect on the way you felt when you worked through the What Does It Really Cost to Live worksheet. Focus on the pain and disappointment you felt when you realized you were trying to live a life you really couldn't afford. Relive the anger and frustration you felt when you had to go back over the worksheet and eliminate so many items that were important to you. Got it? Now bring up Financial Reality #1: Everything turns to junk. Juxtapose the awful feelings of loss from the What Does It Really Cost to Live worksheet exercise and the wonderful feelings of freedom and relief from the financial gargoyle exercise. Nail them together with Financial Reality #1. Hmm.

Is it possible that the pursuit and acquisition of "things" is a stress-producing problem? Does letting go of things bring serenity? If you have done or are doing the exercises, you'll be able to make that decision for yourself. Making decisions for yourself is what becoming a Financial Adult is all about. And that's all I want for you.

Thinking

The emotional difference between an adult and a child is the ability to delay or defer gratification. If we have come from environments where our needs were never met (or where having our needs met was filled with uncertainty), we learned to take care of ourselves. Do it now, take it now, get it now, otherwise you'll never have it. If our parents deprived us, we are likely to respond by indulging ourselves.

Part of financial recovery is learning how to re-parent our financial inner child. Often this part of our inner child has learned that he can get anything in the toy store (whether the "toys" are electronic or sports equipment, clothing, cars, or theater tickets) by simply signing his name on one of those long gray slips of paper. It doesn't take any money and you don't have to wait—credit card companies (and others) advocate "having it all now." Surely they want the best for us, just like the indulgent aunt, grandparent, or fairy godmother when we were growing up. Don't they?

Earlier in the book, I spelled out Rule #1: Pay cash or do without. This is a financial parenting rule designed to create some pain from which a change in thinking and behavior will emerge. Now we are ready for Rule #2: *Think!* The application of this rule is to think about each unplanned purchase *for one hour for each dollar the item costs.*

Here's how it works. I personally have great difficulty not spending money in bookstores or at magazine racks. Bookstores are very "slippery" places for me. Typically, if I see a new recovery title or a computer magazine or something about vintage airplanes, cars, or motorcycles, I get a real excited feeling inside. "I want it now!" (That's my nine-year-old financial inner child acting out.) My financial inner parent must teach my inner child about delayed gratification. That's a parent's job, after all, teaching his child to become an adult. So my parent says to my child, "It's perfectly alright for you to want that $12 book, and (not 'but') if you still want it in twelve hours, you shall have it."

My child feels okay with this. He knows that it's okay to have needs and wants, that he's not being ignored or minimized, that he's not being talked out of or into anything. He makes a connection between the amount of money being spent and time, that little purchases don't require as much thought as larger purchases. The system (rule) is rational and measurable, so it is safe. It is also non-negotiable at both ends (if my child still wants the book in twelve hours, he gets it, no questions asked), so my child feels empowered.

More often than not, once I've left the store, the book, magazine, or necktie has faded from my memory before I even reach my car. My child was happy to have been heard and acknowledged. He gets in the car looking forward to a glass of cold milk at home and maybe some TV. He has grown a little more. Someday soon he will no longer respond to the stimulus of the smell of the bookstore.

Please note that I'm talking only about unplanned purchases. An unplanned purchase is something that you didn't have written down on a list when you left home headed for the store. Obviously, you won't tell the cashier where you just bought $96 worth of groceries that you have to go home and "think about it" for four days. And you won't tell the utility company that you are thinking about paying them. Impulse purchases—and impulse charitable contributions—make up an extraordinary percentage of our total spending.

Think about how often your impulse purchases have been made using credit. Isn't it interesting that credit, the medicator of the pain of financial reality, is always so near to these decisions? Perhaps you can understand the connection between Rule #1, Pay cash or do without, and Rule #2, Think about it for one hour per dollar. You will be an excellent parent to your inner child and to your physical child(ren). Excellent!

Tithing

At a recent lecture, someone in the audience asked me how I had turned my financial life around. An excellent question, I thought, since there were no books, no tapes, no financial counselors at that time. My "MBA Brain," as I refer to it, had gotten me into all my troubles, so it was unlikely that I was going to "brain" my way out.

In the depths of my despair in 1988, I hit bottom. Being completely out of answers, I sought solace in the Bible. (Stay with me—I'm not proselytizing.) I was very comfortable with my relationship with God and with reading and understanding the Bible. It wasn't that I just flipped open the book and started reading, either. I was engaged in a purposeful search for answers in what I believe is God's word. In the book of Malachi (the last book in the Old Testament), Chapter Three, I found what I was looking for—actually, it wasn't what I was looking for at all. It was a challenge from God to take a leap of faith by tithing, giving Him 10 percent of all my earnings. "Please, Lord," I thought to myself, "could we take this leap of faith a little closer to the ground? I'm already broke, y'know." He knew.

But His challenge was connected with a promise: if I brought the whole tithe into his storehouse, He would shower me with such blessings that I would scarcely be able to contain them all. That's what it said, right there in black and white. Well, everything I had come up with wasn't working, so why not try it, I reasoned.

It was very scary at first, giving away 10 percent of the small amounts of money trickling into my life. I'm sure my wife thought I was absolutely certifiable at that point. In hindsight, I am truly amazed at how things worked out! My anxiety level was still high—I thought money would just start pouring in—but somehow the money that came covered only the things we absolutely needed. Often, the money would arrive at the very last minute, frequently from sources that were totally unexpected and unplanned.

God was teaching me how to swim, so to speak, and was showing me that He wouldn't let me drown. Once I caught on to what was happening, my tension level began to drop. He was allowing me to make only enough money from my tax and accounting practice to keep my nose above the water line, but He wouldn't allow me to prosper. I didn't get it. Finally, the pressure of my debts increased until the only way for me to stay afloat was to let go of the now-burdensome practice. I was a drowning man holding onto a bar of gold. I let go.

As I told you in Chapter One, letting go of the company was very difficult, but the same day I signed the closing, I was offered a consulting position. The appointment lasted over a year, paying me over ten times what I had made struggling with my practice in its sixth and final year. The work was both challenging and rewarding. I helped the organization make significant improvements in their financial systems. It was also part-time work, so I had plenty of time to devote to developing my financial counseling and workshops. My large personal debt became manageable while my family and I were able to purchase some of the necessities we had done without for such a long time. I was having fun! I was astounded that I could have fun and make lots of money, too.

I'm not suggesting that tithing is a *quid pro quo* arrangement with God. The Bible says that abundant blessings, not (just) money, are forthcoming. The blessings for me included realizing that I was capable of making, and was worth, large amounts of money with the skills I already possessed. I was able to get in touch with the fact that trust was a major issue for me. Good health abounds in my family. I have time to work on my recovery and I have a supportive wife and kids. I am able to separate myself from my possessions, my work and my money, developing a clearer self-identity. Best of all, I have been guided by God to share my experiences with others through my practice and, in this way, to have my financial needs met. I'm having more fun than ever and I get paid for it! Sometimes it really is too much for me to grasp. Just like the book said.

I've talked to other people who have tithed and hear similar stories from each of them. I have yet to meet anyone who tithes who hasn't had some sort of life-changing experience as a result. I happen to be a Christian, but I am confident that this principle will work for anyone. Regardless of your spiritual beliefs, giving a tenth of the firstfruits of your labor back to the god of your understanding is an exercise in connecting the spiritual and the material. I am certain that it will be an interesting, growthful experience for you. Let me hear about your story.

Our maturation process around money is what this book is all about. Learning to parent our financial inner child is the primary objective. Think for a moment about how a child relates to his possessions. In the beginning, the child is very attached to his things. "Mine" is the descriptor for everything the young child has. Later the child learns to share—another child may touch or even hold, but it's still "mine." Later still, sharing becomes less possessive. Loaning and trading may emerge. Finally, an occasion arises where giving gifts to someone the child likes is required. At first, the child will want to buy his own favorite toy as a gift and will probably have difficulty parting with it. Over time, the child may learn to anticipate what the friend would like and to focus on pleasing the other person. Gifting another person is usually "sold" to the child with the idea that if he gifts his friend, his friend will gift him back. It's still a zero-sum game.

Possessing is a natural act. That is, it's part of our human nature to acquire and have. It's part of our natural survival instinct. But moving from "keeping" to "sharing" to "gifting" is only a social, not spiritual, growth process. Allow me to draw a distinction between "gifting" and "giving." I define gifting as the giving of a gift to someone in exchange for a closer relationship. Notice that, for the child, nothing is actually lost up to this point. If I have received something, such as admiration or adulation, for my gift, then I have simply purchased praise for myself. The "gift" is nothing more than a payment chit or a trigger for a desired response and attention toward me. It is another form of self-gratification.

"Giving," however, is an unnatural act, one reflecting maturity and spiritual growth. Giving is a transcendent experience. Most of the world's spiritual teachings advocate anonymity in giving. This is to separate gifting from giving, the former being a form of psychic or spiritual exchange between human beings, the latter being part of a relationship with God. Givers understand that they are merely conduits for God's love and abundance, much like the garden hose that carries the water from the house to the thirsty flowers. If the receiver of the gift doesn't know who the giver is, there cannot be any emotional repayment. Perhaps the recipient will experience a spiritual awakening as a result, blooming spiritually as the thirsty flowers. This act of "passing it on" is the essence of the Twelfth Step of Alcoholics Anonymous. It is the essence of love and life itself.

In parting, I'd like to assure you that you now have a comprehensive, straightforward program that will bring you to a wonderful new life, free of financial stress and worry. It takes time to get there, of course, but everything I've written absolutely, positively works. If all you get from this book is that you were set up for financial dysfunctionalism before you were even born, that's enough for you to begin changing. And even if you don't see your changes, others will. Everything else here just goes towards shortening the path you'll follow.

I'd love to hear about your experiences. Drop me a line sometime. In the meantime, keep coming back—it works if you work it! God bless you.

About the Author

George Moore, CPA, has unique qualifications for writing this book. Previously overcome by money woes, he has personally experienced the feelings of self-defeat and failure that result from being "hopelessly" in debt. Moore escaped from this trap and has now built a secure life for himself and his family.

Today he is a consultant to business and professional practices and a national speaker and workshop leader in the field of financial recovery and redirection. A frequent guest on TV talk shows, this multi-talented man also writes regular columns for various recovery and self-help newsletters.

He holds memberships in the American Institute of C.P.A.s and the Institute of Management Accountants, as well as serving on the faculty of the Ohio Institute for Addiction Studies. As a Certified Public Accountant, speaker, and financial counselor, he has helped thousands of people overcome mounting financial obligations. Now he shares his wisdom, wit, and winning strategies in *And Forgive Us Our Debts.*

Have a Friend or Colleague Who Needs Help Escaping a Trap?

ORDER FORM

YES, I want ___ copies of *And Forgive Us Our Debts* . . . at $9.95 each, plus $3 shipping per book. (Ohio residents please include $.70 state sales tax.) Canadian orders must be accompanied by a postal money order in U.S. funds. Allow 30 days for delivery.

_____ Check/money order enclosed   *   Charge my ___ VISA ___ MasterCard

Name _____ Phone _____

Organization _____

Address _____

City/State/Zip _____

Card # _____ Expires _____

Signature _____

Check your leading bookstore
or call your credit card order toll free to:
800-860-7600

Please make your check payable and return to:
Cleveland Book Publishers
6000 Lombardo Center, Suite 310
Cleveland, OH 44131-2579